Sports Illustrated
RACQUETBALL

THE SPORTS ILLUSTRATED LIBRARY

BOOKS ON TEAM SPORTS

Baseball	Football: Defense	Ice Hockey
Basketball	Football: Offense	Pitching
Curling: Techniques	Football: Quarterback	Soccer
and Strategy		Volleyball

BOOKS ON INDIVIDUAL SPORTS

Badminton	Judo	Table Tennis
Fly Fishing	*Racquetball	Tennis
Golf	*Running for Women	Track: Running Events
Handball	Skiing	Track: Field Events
Horseback Riding	Squash	Wrestling

BOOKS ON WATER SPORTS

Powerboating	Small Boat Sailing
*Scuba Diving	Swimming and Diving
Skin Diving and Snorkeling	

SPECIAL BOOKS

Dog Training	Training with Weights
Safe Driving	

*EXPANDED FORMAT

Sports Illustrated

RACQUETBALL

BY VICTOR I. SPEAR, M.D.

PHOTOGRAPHS BY HEINZ KLUETMEIER

HARPER & ROW, PUBLISHERS, New York
Cambridge, Philadelphia, San Francisco
London, Mexico City, São Paulo, Sydney

1817

85 9 8 7 6 5
Printed in the United States of America

Photographs on pages 13, 18, 20, 21, 22, 31, 41, 61, 74,
79, 81, 100, 130, 147, 168 by Buck Miller;
photograph on page 23 by Sheedy and Long; photograph
on page 138 by Roger D. Hilbert; cover and
all other photographs by Heinz Kluetmeier.

U.S. Library of Congress Cataloging in Publication Data

Spear, Victor Irwin, birth date
    Sports illustrated racquetball.

    (The Sports illustrated library)
    1. Racquetball. I. Kluetmeier, Heinz.
II. Sports illustrated (Chicago) III. Title.
GV1017.R3S69   796.34   78–27348
ISBN 0-06-015073-4
ISBN 0-06-090954-4 {PBK.}

Contents

Preface

I love this game. If I'm lucky enough to play ten days in a row, excitement still prevails over the prospect of playing the eleventh. I can't get enough. There's never been a sport that offered so much to the average athlete.

I am not a professional, and I won't try to pass myself off as an expert on the techniques of shotmaking. Execution of shots is a science, and for this I have gathered many pearls from the pros to pass along—a composite, a conglomeration, a potpourri. It is the *art* of racquetball that turns me on—the strategy, the manipulation and maneuvers, the chess game. The tactics section is, therefore, personal and innovative—gleaned from tormented hours of searching analysis of how a player with average skills can be a winner.

Redundancy prevails throughout, as it must. You surely won't plow through this as you might an Agatha Christie twister, but will digest it in bits and pieces, going back from time to time to review problem areas. Some points must be made and remade many times so that each minisection may stand alone as an entity.

I trust you will grant me the latitude to refer to the player as *he,* and assume that both he and his opponent are right-handed. The motives

8   are simplicity and clarity—no chauvinism intended. As for you females and southpaws, make the transpositions as you go along. You've been doing it all your lives.

And finally, my sources of inspiration must be recognized. My thanks to Karl von Clausewitz for his treatise on war strategy; to Stephen Potter for his analysis of gamesmanship; to Bobby Fischer for revealing the beauties in checkmate; and to Attila the Hun for his outline of slaughter.

Sports Illustrated
RACQUETBALL

The overhead smash, one of
the many offensive weapons
in the racquetballer's arsenal

1

An Introduction to Racquetball

This country is going bananas over racquetball. In 1972 there were two court clubs in the United States. Now there are more than five hundred, with at least as many more on the drawing boards. The 50,000 players of 1970 have spawned more than 5 million in 1977. Nine years ago only one company made racquetball racquets; now there are nearly a hundred. One company put out 6,000 racquets in 1972; now they are making 50,000 a month. A boom? Explosion would be a better word.

Where's the magic? The reasons abound, but one stands out: Racquetball has the unique combination of being easy to play while offering unlimited challenge for the hearty. How many sports can you jump into and have fun on your first outing? How many games guarantee instant mediocrity?

Racquetball is fun and it's easy. But so are checkers and a Marx Brothers movie. What turns the casual athlete into an addict? The secret is that it can be played on so many different levels. You keep on getting better, almost without trying—first, by learning the geometry of the multiwall bounces, learning to let the ball do some of the running, then by upgrading your shotmaking skills, and finally, by practicing strategy and shot selection until your checkers game is transformed into a chess game, and you are powerless to resist. Easy to play, racquetball is harder to master as artistry, skill, and precision creep into the picture.

It is not expensive, needs no more equipment than would fill your glove compartment, and is free from the spoils of weather. It can be enjoyed at all ages and provides maximum exercise in a minimum of time, and you don't have to chase the ball or lose it.

Racquetball can be simple and it can be complex. It can be leisurely and it can be vigorous. It's cerebral and it's physical. It's finesse and it's power. It's quickness and it's endurance. It's any of these and it's all of these. It can be whatever you want it to be. That's the secret.

Who plays racquetball? Practically everybody. There is no such thing as a typical racquetballer. The game's appeal is universal—it crosses every barrier—its players are men and women, young and old, the physical and the analytical.

Larry Lederman has been an athlete all his life, a dedicated handball player for years. At sixty-two he feels that switching to racquetball will add fifteen years to his four-wall playing time. He loves the game.

Vickie Berry is a fashion model. She used to watch her husband play racquetball. Now she plays and even sweats. And doesn't care who knows it. She loves the game.

Kris Biggs is a seventeen-year-old high-school student. She's neither an academic type nor a social butterfly. She's a jock. And she's hooked on racquetball and plays every day. She eats, sleeps, and dreams four-wall. She loves the game.

Everybody's doing it. The game is making inroads into the lives of many pro athletes, fast catching on as an off-season conditioner because it is a superb stimulus to agility, quickness, and stamina. O. J. Simpson, part owner of a swank racquetball complex in California, finds the game ideal for keeping in shape in the off season. Bud Grant, coach of the Minnesota Vikings, encourages his players to play, and Alan Page and Carl Eller are among the best. Don Coryell, former coach of the St. Louis football Cardinals, owns a racquet club, as does Don Kessinger, formerly of the local baseball contingent.

Ron Cey, Los Angeles Dodger hot third baseman, says, "It's the single most important thing I do to stay in shape. It gives me a good workout in terms of using my reflexes, improves my overall ability to react to the ball, using my wrists, keeping them strong, and holds my weight down."

The glass court. The explosive growth of racquetball is partly owing to the advent of the glass-walled court, which enables spectators to have an intimate view of the action from three sides of the court.

Racket-size comparison (from the left): the rackets used for squash, racquetball, and paddle tennis

Ken Rosewall, who has won just about everything there is to win in tennis, recently grabbed a new headline by winning the Australian racquetball championship at the age of forty-two.

The politicians and show-biz celebrities are also getting into the act. Illinois Governor James Thompson proclaimed an official Racquetball Week in his home state and hides an extra racquet in the company car at all times for emergency purposes. Nobel Prize winner Saul Bellow is turned on. Farrah Fawcett, Shecky Greene, and Wayne Rogers have joined the ranks.

A sport that grew up in the dungeons of the YMCAs and JCCs is now elaborately showcased in highly diversified settings. You'll find courts at seaside resorts, in motels, in civic centers, and in the executive offices of industrial plants. And the longest registration line at University of Iowa is the line signing up for Racquetball 101.

San Diego has been the hot spot of activity from the start. That's where the pros live and where the young aspirants make their pilgrimages in a steady stream. Chicago, St. Louis, Detroit, and Minneapolis are not far behind. Suburban Chicago sports thirty-two racquet clubs, four in little Schaumberg alone. The east coast, somewhat limited in development by high real estate costs, will soon be catching up to what has been a west-coast and midwestern craze until now.

As a business, racquetball is just a dropshot away from being a billion-dollar-a-year industry. Most clubs open their doors from 6:00 A.M. to midnight, seven days a week—and the courts are full. Marketing experts predict that it could surpass tennis in popularity by 1980. From a dollars-and-cents point of view, a court occupies one sixth the space of a tennis court and costs half as much to build.

This is no fad. It's here to stay.

HISTORY

The most fashionable courtside parlor game of the day is to argue the question of who "invented" racquetball. Several claim the title; many are legitimate contributors to the game. I won't be nominating any new candidates for the I-invented-racquetball derby. For, in truth, racquetball never was invented—it evolved. It is the bastard child of racket sports and court games going back hundreds of years. Try to trace a single line of ancestry and you will run into blind alleys. This mongrel branches out in too many directions.

Whether you want to begin with the French game of court tennis of nearly a thousand years ago, the Spanish game of jai alai in the seventeenth century, or the British game of rackets played at the colleges in the early 1800s, the conclusion is the same: Men have had a fascination with the idea of hitting a ball with a weapon for hundreds of years. The variations on the theme are numerous, and it was inevitable that racquetball, as we know it today, be discovered.

The game of handball goes back a thousand years to Ireland and was introduced in the United States by Irish immigrants in the nineteenth century. Who knows how many times during those years players might have experimented with hand tools to swat the ball?

Squash originated in England at the famous Harrow prep school in 1850 and came to the United States some thirty years later.

A major event took place in the 1920s when Earl Riskey of the University of Michigan originated the concept of paddleball (same game, with a solid wood paddle) after watching tennis players practice on a handball court in the off season. Interest mounted slowly, and it wasn't until 1961, about forty years later, that the first National Paddleball Championship Tournament was held in Madison, Wisconsin. A permanent organization was formed in 1962 with Riskey as president.

In the early 1950s Joe Sobek, a squash and tennis pro from the Greenwich, Connecticut, YMCA, began playing paddleball. His tennis background made it obvious to him that the shots would be zippier with a strung racket. A marriage of paddleball, handball, and squash was about to take place, and these are the true ancestors of racquetball. Sobek designed what amounted to a short tennis racket and began to promote the "new" sport, which became known as "paddle rackets." He then set out like an evangelist to gain converts from the ranks of the ancestor sports.

The changes in the game over the next twenty years have involved only the equipment. The court and the rules remain the same. The racquet frame has seen the phasing out of wood (now barred in many places) and the phasing in of aluminum and fiberglass. The ball has been changed many times leading up to today's version—more lively and durable than any preceding ball.

In 1968 a group led by Larry Lederman of the Milwaukee JCC organized the first National Paddle Rackets Tournament in beertown. The players were, for the most part, paddleball buffs swinging rackets. As might be expected, the winner was a former national paddleball champion, Bill Schultz of Madison. The game was beginning to challenge paddleball in popularity, and there was an obvious need for organization and promotion to give structure to the sport. For leadership they turned to Bob Kendler.

Kendler, now seventy-two, was the logical choice. He had the four-wall expertise and experience. He had done it before—with handball. This imaginative genius had fostered and controlled that four-wall sport for several years with a firm hand, and was ready to do the same in paddle rackets. With Kendler you are guaranteed two things—action and controversy—and there were plenty of both.

"Racquetball never was invented—it evolved . . . the bastard child of racket sports and court games going back hundreds of years."

The Birth of the *Qu*

The International Racquetball Association was formed in 1969 under Kendler's guidance. The first order of business was to resolve any confusion between the new game and paddleball. So the name was changed from paddle rackets to racketball. Then with a touch of class the *k* was dropped in favor of *qu*, and snob appeal came to racquetball. Like naming your dog Fido and spelling it "Phaideaux." But it worked. It smacked of uniqueness. With the birth of the *qu* came an identity.

In 1970 Kendler tapped Chuck Leve, a bright University of Miami journalism graduate, to be the executive director of the IRA. Until then, racquetball via the written word could be found only in the handball magazines, squeezed into the rear. Aided by Leve's energy and editorial skills, *Racquetball* magazine was born in 1972, and the sport was picking up steam. Leve is now the editor of *National Racquetball* magazine and a referee of pro tournaments.

But, as noted, where Kendler is, there is conflict. This would prove to be no exception. In the 1950s he had locked horns in a power struggle with AAU's Avery Brundage, and single-handedly wrested control of handball from the old warrior. In the process he had formed the U.S. Handball Association under his own domination. In 1973 a schism developed in the IRA over such things as funding, accounting procedures, and professionalism, and Kendler broke with the organization. He formed the rival U.S. Racquetball Association to sponsor amateur competition, and the National Racquetball Club to govern the freshly organized pro tours. Competition and hard feelings still boil between these and the original IRA. Roles are quite ambivalent in the racquetball world of today, and I won't attempt to unravel the tangle.

When the smoke cleared, Kendler was on top, and he has been a driving force in the growth of racquetball ever since. He standardized it, he organized it, he promoted it—successfully. Ironically, he has never played the game, calling it a "sissy sport" and staying loyal and true to his first love, handball.

The first national racquetball champion was crowned in St. Louis in 1969. He was Bud Meuhleisen, a San Diego dentist who has since given up the practice in favor of his new passion. By 1970, the women had their own division in the IRA. Fran Cohen of St. Louis was the first national champion in 1970. Since then national championships have been held annually, complimented by a steadily growing number of local and regional tournaments throughout the year.

A dedicated player, not wanting to yield good court position, times his leap perfectly to avoid being hit by the ball on its way to the front wall.

THE PROS

Since 1973 there has been a traveling circuit of professional racquetball tournaments. In a sport as new as this, the names keep changing. While none is yet widely known, like a Nicklaus or a Connors, they are not without a color and charisma of their own. Four figures, three men and a woman, stand out:

Marty Hogan, a nineteen-year-old whiz kid from St. Louis, has become a dominant figure on the four-wall scene. In the 1976-77 season he won an astounding nine pro tournaments in a row and topped that feat by his win of the 1978 national championship. It's obvious you'll find no argument on his current number-one ranking. He began playing at age eight and has developed a devastating offensive style, highlighted by a serve clocked at 142 mph. Fearless and brash, his aggressiveness typifies the new wave of racquetball pros.

Charlie Brumfield, a twenty-eight-year-old nonpracticing attorney from San Diego who was the perennial high priest until Hogan came along. Never lacking in ego, Brumfield is referred to by fellow pros as "Silver-Tongue" or "Motor-Mouth," depending on who's listening—a noisy, arrogant, good-humored showman. But most of all—a gamesman. "I am at all times looking for the opportunity within the rules to infuriate my opponent to the point where he can't play as well as he'd like to." A psych artist supreme.

His game is characterized by an intelligent, controlled passing-shot style. When he and Hogan tangle, as is the case in the finals of most tournaments, it is the classic confrontation of the boxer versus the slugger, the strikeout pitcher versus the home-run killer.

Steve Keeley, a twenty-six-year-old nonpracticing veterinarian ("spayed a cat once") from San Diego, is quiet, good-looking, adorned with golden ringlets. Keeley is an authentic original, a rugged individualist who thinks nothing of walking 40 miles to a tournament as he did to one in Michigan, or riding his bike from San Diego to the nationals in St. Louis. A serious, thoughtful, well-honed athlete, he is always near the top as a player, and has become best known as a prolific author and spokesman for the sport.

The last two national women's championships have been won by *Shannon Wright,* a twenty-two-year-old spitfire from San Diego, whose game is characterized by Hoganesque aggressiveness. She threatens to dominate the female side of the sport as Hogan dominates the men. But there is a hungry pack of hotshots on her trail. Peggy Steding, Jennell Marriot, and Kathy Williams all play a ferocious game. Peggy, at forty-two, has been a top player for years. A housewife from Odessa, Texas, she didn't start playing the game

until she was thirty-five; then she proceeded to string out five years of tournament play without losing a single match. Kathy, a former Central Michigan all-around athlete, talented in tennis, swimming, basketball, volleyball, and track, became the first woman manager-pro of a racquetball club, in Livonia, Michigan.

Premier pro Marty Hogan displays his unique style in a variety of ways that would make the teacher of classic form cringe. But who's going to argue with the best player in the world, who can crank, coil, and unleash enormous power with every shot while maintaining pinpoint accuracy? The last photo is the usual result.

Five-time national champ Charlie Brumfield, racquetball's cerebral nonpareil, pauses to acknowledge the gallery

Steve Keeley, pro, author, and spokesman, shown illustrating his characteristic economy of movement in court coverage

Don't ever miss a chance to see the pros in action. It's the greatest show on earth. Pure entertainment. The action is furious, the "gets" spectacular. Of course, you may have the urge to go home and burn your racquet afterwards, but don't we all want to sell our golf clubs after seeing Jack Nicklaus follow up a 300-yard drive with a putting stroke displaying the delicacy of an eye surgeon?

EQUIPMENT

One of the nice surprises to the racquetball beginner is that it's not expensive compared to other sports. You don't have to mortgage the house and car before you set foot on a court. A T-shirt, shorts, and an old pair of sneakers—you're dressed. Rent a racquet for fifty cents, buy a ball for a dollar; you're ready to play racquetball. You can keep it simple because it *is* simple. But once you've been smitten with the passion, you will tend to invest a bit more; you'll want some of the accessories as well as the luxury of owning your own racquet.

The Racquet

The Grip—either leather or rubber. Either is acceptable, and the difference is noted only by the experienced player. Rubber tends to slip more readily when wet and also wears out faster. But the difference is slight. Far more important is the choice of grip *size*. Standard circumference has long been in the 4 ⅛-to-4 ⅝-inch range. The current trend is definitely toward a smaller grip, and the sub-4-inch models are catching on. The larger grips are to be avoided. This will feel somewhat foreign to the tennis player, but will permit a more fluid wrist snap, which is a prerequisite to the racquetball stroke. Above all, go for comfort.

Racquetball racquets (from the left): the obsolete wood frame and the modern aluminum and fiberglass frames

The Frame—either <u>metal</u> (usually aluminum) <u>or fiberglass</u> (plastic). Here again the difference is not crucial. Fiberglass is more breakable but provides more "feel" to the sophisticated player. The old bulky wooden frames are obsolete for well-deserved reasons and are banned in many places. Graphite has also come into play but is often unjustifiably expensive.

The Strings—<u>generally nylon. The tension should be in the range of 24–28 pounds,</u> as compared to 50–55 pounds in a tennis racket. The pros will occasionally stray outside the normal range for reasons most of us wouldn't appreciate. If a string breaks, restringing is a simple task at most clubs.

Length, Width, and Shape—the sum of the length and the width not to <u>exceed 27 inches, according to the rules.</u> This allows the player the option of having a bit more length (usually an inch) while sacrificing the same in width, resulting in a more oblong racquet. The pros go both ways on this.

The Wrist Thong—mandatory, so don't get any idea of switching hands to avoid a backhand.

In summary, don't lie awake nights in torment over which style racquet to use. The choice will have little effect on your play until you reach top levels of competition. Happily, the weapons have become so standardized that the differences are hazy, to say the least.

The Ball

The ball is much like a tennis ball without the fuzz. It is hollow rubber, 2 ¼ inches in diameter, weighs 1.4 ounces, and has a pressure of 2–4 pounds. The differences between brands of balls can be extreme, especially in the liveliness of the bounce, which can vary so much that it can dictate the entire strategy of the game. In tournament play, the choice of ball is not yours but is made by the directors, and the ball's action may vary anywhere from dull to super-lively. If you are planning to enter a tournament, it behooves you to find out in advance which make of ball is being used. Then play your practice matches with the same make. I hope the day is not far off when all balls will be standardized to nearly the same bounce.

The Glove

The glove, of course, is optional, though I can't imagine playing without one. There are a few blessed players who don't sweat more than a dewdrop. For most of us, a thin leather glove, similar to a golf glove, is the answer to poor grip control in a sweaty paw. But some players would rather hook a minitowel over their shorts than wear a glove.

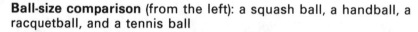

Ball-size comparison (from the left): a squash ball, a handball, a racquetball, and a tennis ball

Sweatbands

A glove stays dry only so long, then needs to be changed as it gets so wet that its grip begins to fail. This can be delayed by wearing an absorbent sweatband on the wrist, to catch the rivulets of sweat running down the arm before they get onto the glove. The same principle may be applied to the head. Wear a stretchable, absorbent headband around the forehead to keep your eyes clear.

Clothing

Wear whatever turns you on, baby. The traditional white shorts and T-shirt are being upstaged of late by color-coordinated outfits that would rival the tennis frocks of Christian Dior. Rules are also less stringent; dark colors are allowed in places where they used to be verboten. Warmup suits and sweat pants are also growing in popularity, particularly among those who have no love for the multicolored welts caused by shots that hit players instead of walls. Doubles teams should help the referee by wearing similar clothing.

Eyeguards and Protective Glasses

Means of protecting the eyes ought to be mandatory, but it will take a few thousand more squashed eyeballs to make it so. The controversy parallels the ancient debate over the wrist thong. "It's safer, but it impedes my play." The difference here is that the motivation ought to be much more acute, for in this case you are protecting *yourself.* The wrist thong is to protect the other player from a flying racquet. Studies indicate that 5 percent of all four-wall players

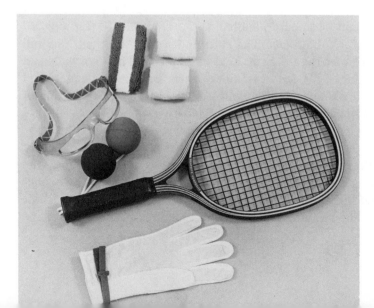

Accessory equipment: optional wrist bands, headband, eyeguard, and glove shown along with the basic essentials (the racquet is graphite)

sustain some form of eye injury during play, some resulting in permanent damage; detached retina, scarred cornea, and even blindness. Not only will you be more secure wearing eyeguards, but you'll be a better player because you won't be so reluctant to watch the ball right through to the moment of contact.

If you wear glasses, be sure to use those with unbreakable or shatter-proof lenses. Or try contact lenses with eyeguards.

Shoes

Spend the time you've saved on racquet selection in choosing a good-quality pair of shoes that fit. The quality is usually reflected in the form-fitting heel support and curvature. The wear and tear on the feet in this game—destructive enough under optimal conditions—are compounded by wearing ill-fitting shoes with poor support. High-top shoes provide nothing more than an illusion of ankle support, so don't bother with these. If you're prone to sprains, wrap firmly with an elastic bandage.

Socks

Two pairs of socks will provide extra protection from blisters.

As you can see, the subject of equipment and dress is becoming ever more complicated as the sport grows in popularity. I'm not a better player than I was five years ago, but it takes me ten more minutes to get dressed.

THE GAME

Racquetball is played on a standard handball court, enclosed, 40 feet long, 20 feet wide, and 20 feet high. Basic handball rules and scoring are used. The ball is slightly larger and softer than the one used in handball. The four walls and ceiling are usually made of plaster, wood-fiber panels, or poured concrete and the floor of wood. All six surfaces are used in play, but the upper portion of the back wall is left open for spectator and referee viewing. Glass walls are coming into vogue as public interest keeps on growing.

Racquetball is a game of alternate hits. The object is to return each shot to the front wall before the ball has bounced on the floor a second time. One player stands in the serving zone, usually near the center, and serves by bouncing the ball once and then hitting it toward the front wall. The serve must hit the front wall first, then rebound far enough in the air to pass the short line

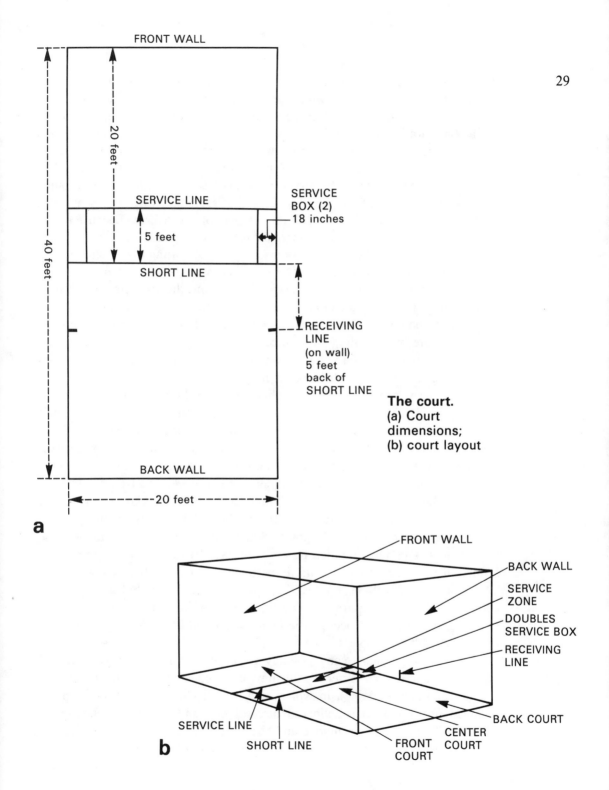

The court.
(a) Court dimensions; (b) court layout

(a) labels: FRONT WALL, 20 feet, 40 feet, SERVICE LINE, SERVICE BOX (2), 18 inches, 5 feet, SHORT LINE, RECEIVING LINE (on wall) 5 feet back of SHORT LINE, BACK WALL, 20 feet

(b) labels: FRONT WALL, BACK WALL, SERVICE ZONE, DOUBLES SERVICE BOX, RECEIVING LINE, BACK COURT, CENTER COURT, FRONT COURT, SHORT LINE, SERVICE LINE

before hitting the floor—but not so far as to hit the back wall before it hits the floor. After hitting the front wall, the ball may carom off one side wall on its way to the floor and still be a legal serve. If it hits a second side wall, the ceiling, or the back wall before the floor, it is a "fault." The server is given a second chance without penalty. If he serves two consecutive faults he loses the serve.

If the serve falls in legally, but the receiver's view of the ball is obstructed by the position of the server, a "screen" serve is called. This amounts to a no-fault serve, and the server is allowed to serve again without penalty. It used to be strictly a judgment call on the part of the referee. Because of the number of disputes, however, a better definition was needed. A recent amendment to the rules clarifies the situation somewhat by stating that a screen serve must be ruled if the ball passes within 18 inches of the server's body.

The receiver must stand at least 5 feet behind the short line, but it is to his advantage to be 10–15 feet back. He must return the serve to the front wall before it has bounced on the floor a second time. He has the option of hitting it either before or after the first bounce. His shot may then go directly to the front wall or ricochet off any combination of walls and ceiling on its way—as long as it hits the front wall before it hits the floor.

The server then has the same challenge, and the rally is on. The first to fail loses the exchange. Points may be scored only by the server (as in volleyball and badminton). If the server loses the exchange, he loses the serve but loses no points. The other player then has a chance to score points on his own serve. The server keeps the serve as long as he wins the rallies.

Racquetball games have traditionally been played to 21 points; tournament matches decided on two out of three games. Many variations in scoring this young sport are being tried in an effort to keep large tournaments moving. Some games are shortened to 15 points. Some matches are decided on one game to 31 points. The most popular system is to have two games to 21 points and a third, if necessary, to 11 points. Experiments will undoubtedly continue.

Simple? Of course. That is, if the players would politely leave the room between shots—or be separated by a net partition, as in the more civilized game of tennis. But, alas, they occupy the same area, often literally, which brings us to the very difficult subject of "hinders."

Tennis opponents can't possibly get in each other's way. Racquetball players can and do. The referee's dilemma is to judge whether the obstruction is accidental (unavoidable), in which case the play is stopped and the point replayed; or if the block is deliberate or careless (avoidable), in which case the referee calls an avoidable hinder and the rally is forfeited. In a rat-a-tat-tat exchange rally, this can be a very difficult distinction to make and often leads

Hinder. The irresistible force has met the immovable object on his way to the ball. The point is played over. (Brumfield and McCoy)

Hazard. In this potentially dangerous situation, the rear player is crowding too closely and risks being struck by his opponent's racquet on follow-through.

to heated argument. And if it's difficult in singles, imagine how much worse it is in a doubles game with eight arms, eight legs, four bodies, and four racquets on the court.

Play is also stopped on a hinder call if a shot strikes the other player on the way to the front wall, if the ball breaks, or if the ball flies over the back wall after hitting the front wall. All this can be quite complicated. Refer to the rules for further clarification of hinders.

Racquetball can be a dangerous game if played by wild men who flail about with no regard for their opponents' bodies. Although hinder calls are usually made to ensure fairness in scoring, an even more important purpose is to ensure survival into tomorrow. In this regard, a few gentle hints are in order:

1. Always avoid hitting the other player with the ball—or, more especially, with your racquet—by holding your shot when necessary. Be aware of his position at all times.

2. Don't plow into him to get at the ball. If you're blocked, a hinder should be called and the point replayed.

3. Work on attaining the proper angle of follow-through when stroking your shots, so as to avoid hitting your opponent with a roundhouse swing *after* hitting the ball. Tennis players will have to adjust to a slightly more upward follow-through arc.

4. Never hit the ball after the point is ended. Freak accidents occur when a player strikes a shot in anger after missing the previous one. The other player, having won the rally, is usually not paying attention any longer.

5. Never argue a safety hinder called by your opponent, even if it's a mite shady. Get down on bended knee and thank him for saving your life. Be willing to replay any point clouded with doubt.

So let us embark on a racquetball odyssey, of sorts. Throughout these pages I will dissect all aspects of the game, from serving to psyching, with a few pearls on conditioning and practice thrown in for good measure. Included will be discussions of all the shots in the game and their appropriate responses. I will also attempt to outline and develop a basic winning strategy, and then branch out into the modifications needed to cope with the various styles of play.

Innocent, unsuspecting reader: Prepare yourself to be hooked by this game. It's a grabber.

2

Strokes and Shots: The Fundamentals

This section will be brief, and as simple as possible. This is not the place to learn how to hit a racquetball shot. An hour on the court with a good teacher is worth far more. Don't try to learn shooting technique out of a book—any book. Strategy, yes, but technique, never. The purpose of this material is to load your emergency kit, to store away, as a reference source, something to dust off and review when things go sour. Fundamentals have a way of getting ragged from time to time, and it may be necessary to go back to the ABC's to show up your mistakes, and what *not* to do. Don't take this for negative thinking; on occasion it can be useful to approach a problem in reverse—to eliminate errors systematically in the search for excellence.

To execute the shots of racquetball, you need to learn three basic hitting motions: the forehand, the backhand, and the overhead. The forehand stroke is used on shots on your "racquet side" of the court, the backhand on shots to your "free-hand side," and the overhead on high shots. As we proceed with a detailed description of each, be sure to note the fundamental principles of grip, body action, and follow-through that apply to all three.

33

34

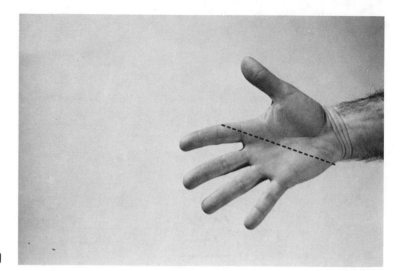

a

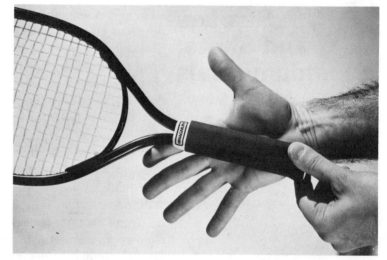

b

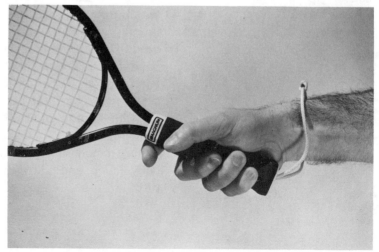

c

The forehand grip.
(a) First, imagine a diagonal line from the inner heel of your hand to the first joint of the index finger; then (b) place the racquet handle on this line, (c) close the hand, and slide the index finger up a bit. (d) Notice how a V has been formed over the racquet. (e) The index or "trigger" finger is in the proper position.

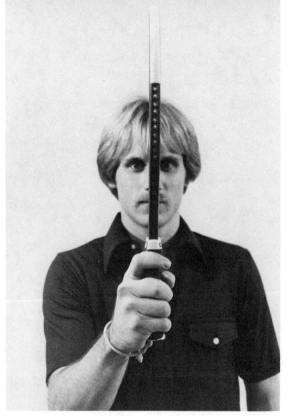

e

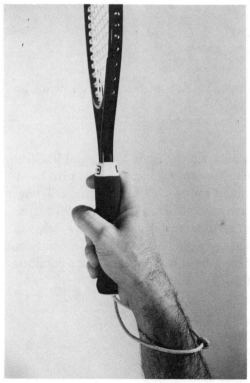

d

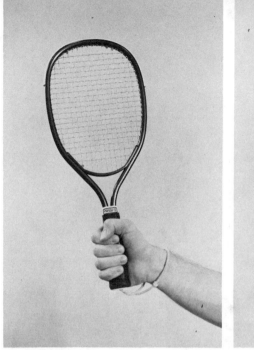 

a   **b**

Common errors in the grip: (a) fist grip; (b) eagle claw; (c) stranglehold; (d) index-finger extension

THE STROKES

The Forehand

Let's analyze the forehand stroke in three stages: the grip, the backswing, and the hit.

The Grip

To grip the racquet, open your hand, palm up. Imagine a diagonal line from inner "heel" point to the first knuckle of the index finger. Lay the grip handle next to the line and close your hand. Extend your curled index ("trigger") finger slightly upward toward the neck for better control. Turn the racquet 90 degrees, and you should see a V formed by your thumb and index finger—what the tennis pros call "shaking hands with the racquet." Grip the racquet firmly but not tightly. (No death grip but no wet fish either.) It should feel like a comfortable, controlled extension of your hand.

Here are some common errors in the grip:

Fist grip—no trigger-finger control
Eagle claw—too low on the handle

c   **d**

Stranglehold—too high on the handle

Index-finger extension—a definite no-no (I've never understood how some golfers can putt with this grip, either.)

The Backswing

To arrive at the correct hitting position, you must initiate the backswing properly. This requires doing three things at once:

1. Pivot slightly more than 90 degrees from the face-front position so as to be facing the side wall after you draw your right foot back. Feet should be a comfortable 12–18 inches apart, nearly shoulder width.

2. Bring the racquet back with elbow bent 90 degrees. Your weight should shift to the back foot.

3. Cock your wrist at head height, pointing right at your ear.

You'll be surprised to find the backswing much closer in style to a golf backswing than to the tennis stroke. But here the "flying elbow" that you golfers have spent years to control is not only permissible but necessary. Practice getting the backswing down pat. You must learn to execute all three steps simultaneously, with a relaxed, fluid motion.

Here are some common errors in the backswing:

Failure to take a full pivot
Failure to bend the elbow 90 degrees
Failure to cock the wrist
Failure to bring the racquet up to head height

The Hit

For the hit as for the backswing, you also begin the downswing with lower body action, rather than the arm. The first move is a small step forward with the left foot, shifting your weight forward off the back foot as a baseball hitter and a golfer does. Drive your knees, hips, and body through the shot as you swing the racquet forward. Just before contact, 6 inches from the ball, uncock your wrist with a healthy snap. This will seem quite foreign to tennis players schooled in the art of the stiff wrist. You should hear a definite "whoosh" sound at the wrist snap when practicing without the ball.

Follow through naturally with a slight upward arc. You don't have to force the follow-through consciously—you'd actually have to use force to prevent it. Just *let* it happen.

a

b

c

Forehand stroke. (a) The player begins the pivot with a hip turn; (b) the racquet is brought back, the arm bent 90 degrees at the elbow, the wrist cock begins; (c) the wrist is now fully cocked as the weight is shifted forward with a small step; (d) the front foot is firmly planted as the strong lower-body action leads the swing through (note the elbow precedes the wrist to allow for a wrist snap); (e) contact is made parallel with the front foot with arm now fully extended and wrist snapping through; (f) a full follow-through completes the stroke.

d

e

f

The power of the stroke is generated primarily by two factors: the driving weight shift and the wrist snap. The actual arm swing provides little by comparison. The moment of truth, of course, is the instant the racquet makes contact with the ball. All that goes before is useless if two requirements are not met at impact:

1. The face of your racquet must be perfectly square to the target. Everything up to this point is designed to achieve this. Don't turn your racquet over the top, and don't undercut the ball.

2. The contact must be made opposite your forward foot. A normal forehand passing shot should be struck at knee-high level. A kill shot should be hit just above ankle height. You must wait for the ball to drop before the hit. Pro Marty Hogan goes through from fifteen to twenty racquets a year, breaking them on the floor while trying to contact the kill shot at ever lower points.

Here are the most common errors in the forehand hit:

Failure to shift weight and step into the shot
Making contact too high (above the knee)
Making contact too far back (off the right foot)
Turning the racquet face over the ball at impact

a   **b**

Wrist snap. The blur indicates the speed and power generated by the wrist snap just before the hit.

Point of contact (opposite). Both of these shots are hit when the ball is even with the front foot. Stroke the ball (a) just below the knee for a passing shot, (b) ankle high for a kill shot.

Now that's a follow-through—and not a bad weight shift, either.

Grip shift: (a) the forehand grip; (b) the backhand grip: slide the thumb "down under" and rotate the trigger finger slightly over the top.

The Backhand

For a backhand, the first thing you have to do is adjust the grip—a slight counterclockwise rotation to the left. The trigger finger slides over the top a bit and the thumb down under—no more than a wiggle. Don't exaggerate the shift. The purpose is to ensure a square hit on contact. Without the adjustment, the racquet face is slightly open and would cause an undercut floater. At first, the grip shift will be a nuisance; later it will be unconscious and automatic. You might find it useful to use the free hand as a guide, but the modern two-handed tennis backhand is not used in racquetball.

Once you've made the grip rotation, the entire stroke is almost a mirror image of the forehand:

1. The pivot
2. The backswing with elbow bent 90 degrees
3. The wrist cock
4. The forward step
5. The weight shift
6. The leaning in of the lower body
7. The forward swing
8. The wrist snap
9. The hit
10. The follow-through

a

b

a   **b**   **c**

Backhand stroke. (a) Begin the ready position, knees slightly bent, weight forward off the heels, body mobile; (b) the hip turn and pivot initiate the backswing; (c) the racquet is taken back with arm bent almost 90 degrees at the elbow, and the wrist cock begins; (d) the wrist is now fully cocked as a step forward leads the weight shift; (e) contact will be made with the arm fully extended and the wrist snapping through parallel to the front foot (eyes never leave the ball); (f) a full follow-through completes the stroke

Backhand stroke (from above), showing the same features as the previous sequence but from a different angle: (a) the hip turn; (b) the full pivot, nearly 135 degrees (more exaggerated than the forehand pivot); (c) the backswing and wrist cock; (d) the forward step and weight shift leading the hit; (e) the follow-through

a   **b**   **c**

d

e

f

d

e

Exaggerated wrist cock.
Unorthodox but effective for pro
Craig McCoy. His backhand is
initiated by an "overcocked" wrist
coil. It works for him, so he stays
with it.

Besides the obvious, there are also a few minor differences between this stroke and the forehand. Your pivot should be slightly exaggerated, nearly a three-quarter turn so as to be facing the rear corner rather than the side wall. The contact should be made at a slightly more forward point than the forehand —opposite the toe rather than opposite the instep. And finally, it's best to make contact just above the ankle on a backhand kill shot, not quite so low as with the forehand kill.

I can't think of a more appropriate spot for a comment on unorthodoxy. Don't sell it short. Classic form play is best for *most* players. But there are exceptions to the rule. There are those few players who would simply ruin their game if they forcibly limited themselves to conventional form. The wide variety of stances in great baseball hitters will attest to this—and who is going to be the one to tell Jack Nicklaus that his flying right elbow is "wrong"? I know a topnotch racquetball player who hits his backhand stroke with the forehand side of the racquet. He rotates the racquet a full 180 degrees—*palm side* facing the front wall. And he's a great shooter! What's more, he has a brother and two sisters who hit the same stroke, and all with effectiveness and control. It must be in their genes. We all should have learned by now that there's more than one way to skin a cat.

The Overhead

For the overhead, the grip is the forehand grip. The stroke is similar to the motion of a tennis serve—not a direct overhead square shot, but more of an over-the-shoulder three-quarter motion—like throwing a baseball. The racquet face is turned slightly inward at impact. The pivot and weight shift are less pronounced, but some lower body action is necessary. Don't hit this shot, or any shot, from a flat-footed, stiff-legged stance. Bend the knees and rotate your hips as you go into your backswing. Then move your body forward through the shot as you swing at the ball. The follow-through arc is first upward and forward, then downward and across. The contact is made slightly above the head and forward as you lean into the front foot.

The high backhand ceiling shot isn't actually hit with an overhead, but more of a shoulder-high sweep that goes upward and across. The other elements of the backhand stroke remain the same.

a

b

The overhead. (a) The knees are bent and the pivot is less pronounced than in the backhand or forehand; (b) the racquet is back as the heels leave the floor and the forward weight shift begins; (c) the arm is fully extended at contact and all the weight is forward; (d) the follow-through completes the stroke.

c

d

Backhand ceiling stroke. (a) The pivot begins; (b) the racquet is back and the forward step is taken; (c) the hit takes place about chest high rather than "overhead"; (d) the follow-through completes the stroke.

c

d

Back-Wall Play

The subject of back-wall play must be treated under its own heading, even though we are still dealing with the same basic forehand and backhand strokes. What makes it unique is that the ball is traveling *toward* the front wall when you hit it. Can you imagine trying to hit a baseball pitched from behind you? New players invariably find this the most difficult part of the game. The difficulty is in the footwork and timing rather than the swing. It's a challenge

d   **c**

Back-wall play, forehand. (a) The
key to back-wall play is to follow
the flight of the ball with eyes *and*
body, using the sideways shuffle; (b)
set up into a good hitting position;
(c) wait for the ball to drop into the
proper hitting area; (d) finish the
stroke with a full follow-through.

b

a

Back-wall play, forehand (from above). Note how the player waits until the ball is even with the front foot before making the hit.

to gauge your setup so as to be in the hitting position when the ball reaches the hitting area. Here are a few dos and don'ts:

1. Move with the ball as it goes to the back wall and forward again. Don't just make a guess and stand there waiting for it to come back to you.

2. Use a sideways shuffle as you retreat. Don't turn your back or backpedal.

3. You won't have to pivot much on the backswing. If you use a sideways shuffle, you're already facing the side wall.

a **b**

4. Adhere to the fundamental hitting area—off the *front* foot. Don't make contact too far back simply because the ball is coming from that direction. You have to let the ball actually pass you a second time before you hit it.

5. Don't make contact too high. Letting the ball drop to the knee and ankle levels is still appropriate. One of the most common errors in back-wall play is striking the ball waist-high off the back foot. Keep your center of gravity low by breaking down at the knees and the waist. This makes it easier to make split-second adjustments of your position relative to the ball.

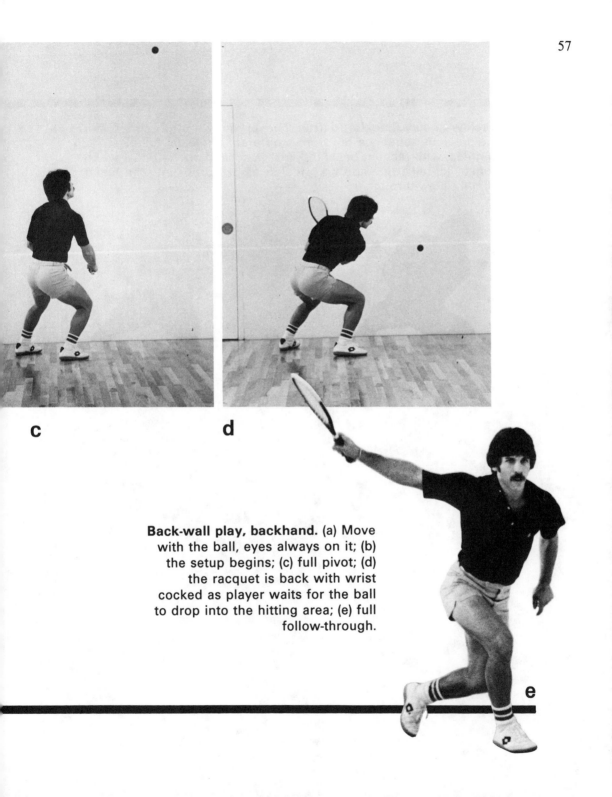

c

d

Back-wall play, backhand. (a) Move
with the ball, eyes always on it; (b)
the setup begins; (c) full pivot; (d)
the racquet is back with wrist
cocked as player waits for the ball
to drop into the hitting area; (e) full
follow-through.

e

Back-wall play, backhand (from above), showing the same features as the previous sequence but from a different angle: (a) full pivot, 135 degrees, with racquet back; (b) wrist is cocked, lower body action begins; (c) full stride and weight shift as ball drops into the hitting area; (d) full follow-through

a

b

c   **d**

OFFENSIVE SHOTS

Once you've learned the three basic strokes, you can start having fun. Step inside a court and flail away. As the ball bounds and rebounds off the six surfaces of that concrete shoe box, you'll be fascinated by the endless possibilities. But all you've learned thus far are the motions. The next step is to learn the objectives of the various racquetball shots and where to aim the ball to achieve these objectives. The variations in shotmaking are almost infinite. A few of the most basic weapons for your arsenal follow.

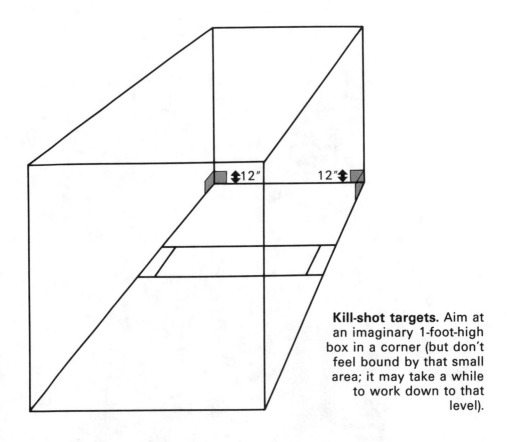

Kill-shot targets. Aim at an imaginary 1-foot-high box in a corner (but don't feel bound by that small area; it may take a while to work down to that level).

The Kill Shot

The kill shot is the shot you hit as low on the front wall as possible—without hitting the floor first. It qualifies as a kill if the other player can't get up to it before the second bounce. The perfect kill hits barely above the floor and literally rolls back out—a "rollout"—permitting no possible return. In real life, such perfection rarely happens. Most of us mortals aim 6–12 inches above the floor to allow a little room for error.

Aim your kill shots dead into the corner. You'll seldom hit right into the angle—"crotch"—and the result will be a random mixture of three variations.

Straight Kill—the ball hits the front wall and rebounds straight out, parallel to the side wall, without touching it.

Pinch Shot—the ball brackets the corner by hitting the side wall, then the front wall, before the floor.

The perfect kill shot: knees bent, weight low, ball hit just off the floor, strong follow-through

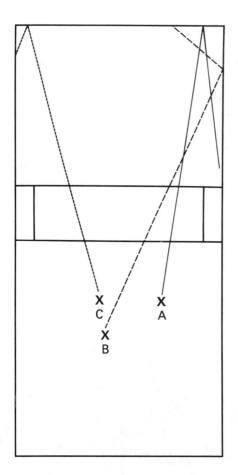

Kill-shot variations. (A) Straight-out kill; (B) Side-wall–front-wall kill; (C) Front-wall–side-wall kill

Reverse Pinch—same as the pinch shot, but hits the front wall first.

When you reach higher levels of play, you'll be able to execute with enough precision to separate the above into three distinct shots, chosen on the basis of position. This is unrealistic for most players. They would be better off to shoot for the corner every time and let the results be a random mixture of the three. It's far more important to concentrate on the *height* of the shot, and to be able to execute from either side to either corner.

The potential errors on kill shots are obvious. If the shot is hit too low, it won't make it to the front wall before hitting the floor. This results in that sickening squeak known as a "skip-ball," and the rally is lost. If it's hit too high, the ball rebounds all the way back to mid-court for an easy setup.

The court has a side-to-side dimension of 20 feet. One step and a wingspan won't cover the whole court, even for the quickest of players. If you can hit the ball past your opponent, you may win the point. You usually have two choices: passing him on the same side of the court you're hitting from ("down-the-wall pass") or passing him on the other side ("cross-court pass"). In either case, the ball must be hit sharply enough to pass him and low enough (usually knee to waist-high on the front wall) not to hit the back wall before the second bounce. If it's too high, it rebounds off the back wall for an easy get. The angle

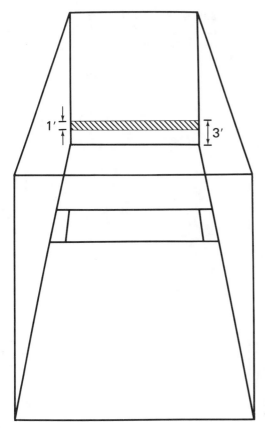

Passing-shot target zone—a 1-foot horizontal band reaching no more than 3 feet high on the front wall

must be wide enough to outreach him but not so wide as to hit the side wall too early. This would cause the ball to rebound toward center court rather than pass him. Whether you need to hit the side wall at all depends on his position. The specific angles can't be verbalized, but one generalization can be made on a geometric basis: If you are hitting a shot from one side of the court and attempting to pass your opponent on the other side (cross-court pass), your front-wall target will be very close to dead center. Most cross-court passing shots should be aimed at the center of the front wall. You have to go out on the court and hit a few to find out.

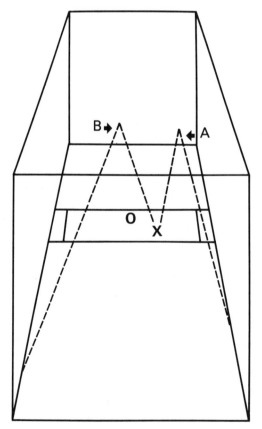

Passing-shot variations.
Catching the opponent (O) out of position (too far forward), the player (X) has the option of (A) the down-the-wall pass or (B) the cross-court pass.

The Ceiling Shot

You can't score a point on every shot. But you'd like a chance to score on the next shot, or the next. To get that second chance, you have to stop the other guy from scoring by giving him a difficult shot and position. The ceiling shot is the best way to guarantee that you'll have at least one more chance to hit the ball.

The first time I heard about this shot I couldn't believe it. It seemed ridiculous to use the ceiling for anything other than keeping out the rain. In 1971 I hadn't yet been exposed to the new live ball. I was not yet aware that my beloved lob shot was about to go the way of the horse and buggy. The live ball made it too difficult to control the depth of the lob shot. The game needed a new defensive stopper. The ceiling shot was the answer.

This shot is usually hit from back court. Front-court situations normally call for more offensive responses. Hit the ball toward the front wall–ceiling junction so as to strike the ceiling first, about 3 feet short of the crotch. The ball will then hit the front wall, bound down to the floor in the service area, and arch softly into the back court.

Once you get the hang of it, you define your goal more sharply. The specific purpose is to force a shoulder-high backhand return from deep in the left corner. You learn by practice just how hard and how high to hit the shot in order to gain the proper depth. If it's too shallow, it's a sure setup. If it's too deep, it rebounds off the back wall and may be a setup.

When you've mastered the depth, then shift your attention to angle. Try to hit the shot close enough toward the corner to make it hug the side wall throughout its return course ("wallpaper ball"). It's more risky but a much better shot if it works, compared to concentrating on depth alone. The risk is that if the angle is too sharp into the corner, the ball will rebound off the side wall for a mid-court setup. But if you hit it just right, your intended defensive shot might turn out to be a surprise winner, every bit as good as a rollout kill shot. The wallpaper ball is the only shot in the game that can make a good player whiff. (The only way to return a perfect wallpaper ball is to scrape your racquet along the wall as you make contact with the ball.)

You must learn to hit a ceiling shot with both backhand and forehand. But this is the only situation wherein it's kosher to hit a forehand (overhead) stroke on the backhand side of the court. If you have more confidence in the forehand and enough room away from the left wall, go right ahead. No demer-

The player on the left awaits a ceiling shot with racquet back and knees bent. Notice how his opponent has moved to the center-court area, where she will be in the best position to handle his return.

its. You have plenty of time to get back into good position. Even the pros do it. The backhand ceiling shot is definitely more difficult to execute. Of course a perfect ceiling shot won't allow you the option. If it hugs the left wall, there's no way you can hit it forehand.

The Drive Shot

The drive shot is a passing shot by another name. It carries a different label if you have little chance to pass your opponent for an outright winner. The more modest intent here is a defensive one, to drive him into the back court for his next shot while you capture center-court control (discussed in the strategy section). Passing shots can be used for both offensive and defensive purposes. Kill shots cannot; they are strictly offensive.

The drive shot is usually driven cross-court and aimed to hit the front wall about 2–3 feet high. It should be angled to hit the side wall at hip height at the same court depth as the other player. If he tries to hit it in the air as it rebounds toward him, he'll have a difficult kill shot. If he lets it pass, his next shot will be from deep in the back court.

Ceiling-shot target zone. The ball should strike the ceiling first, approximately 3 feet short of the front wall.

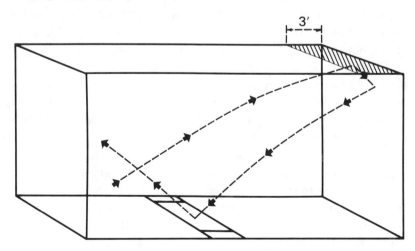

Z-ball target. The ball should strike the front wall first, approximately 3 feet from the corner and 3 feet below the ceiling.

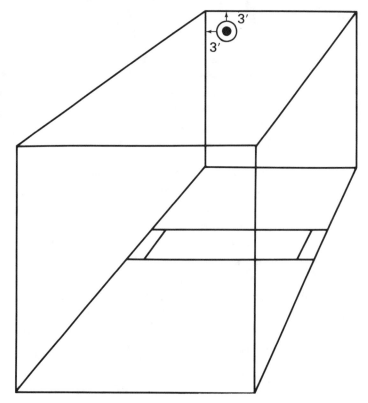

The Z-Ball

The Z-ball is the exotic. Every game has one. Football has its flea-flicker, baseball its suicide squeeze, golf its upside-down-left-handed-5-iron-next-to-the-tree shot. When you hit this one to perfection, you feel like standing back and applauding yourself. The Z-ball also came into being along with the live ball. It takes too much brute strength to hit it with a dead one.

As the name suggests, the ball travels in three directions, off three walls. But the most important one is the last. If hit correctly, it spins crazily off the third wall at a surprising 90-degree angle, *parallel* with the back wall. If it is deep enough, it will crawl along the back wall in a way that makes it nearly impossible to get a racquet face behind it. If a side-wall wallpaper ball is tough to hit, imagine its counterpart on the back wall, going east to west.

The key to this shot is your court position. Don't try it if you're deeper than three-quarter court. That position will not give you enough angling for the ball to rebound into the second side wall *before* the back wall. If it hits the back wall before the second side wall, it isn't a Z-ball. It won't have the desired sidespin and will pop forward for an easy setup.

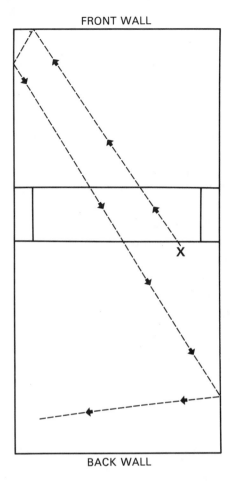

FRONT WALL

BACK WALL

Path of the Z-ball. The ball rebounds sharply off the front wall into the side wall, then carries diagonally into the back court, "jumping" off the second side wall with surprising sidespin.

The best spot to try a Z-ball from is near the short line in the off-center position, not far from the side wall. This shot must be hit hard. Aim at a target high on the front wall, about 3 feet from the side-wall crotch in the opposite corner. Hit the shot high, but don't catch the ceiling. It should carom off the front wall to the side wall and then rebound diagonally to the opposite rear corner. If it then hits the second side wall before the floor, ceiling, or back wall, you've got yourself a shot. It may leave your opponent nothing but a reverse back-wall smash for a return. If it's pinpoint perfect, he won't have even that. As with a perfect ceiling shot, this defensive shot can turn out to be a winner —if it's good enough.

One warning—don't get trapped out of position by your own shot. It's easy to be hypnotized into paralysis by the flight of a Z-ball. The shot will often return close to the point of origin. If you fail to get back to center court after you stroke the ball, you'll soon find yourself boxed out.

The Around-the-Wall Ball (AWB)

The around-the-wall ball is a multiwall shot that differs from the Z-ball in several respects. It has the same general path, cross-court to the corner and back again. But the object is to hit the side wall *before* the front wall. The dynamics of the angle and spin then cause the ball to bounce off the second side wall with overspin rather than 90-degree sidespin.

In contrast to the Z-ball, this shot is best hit from back court. Hit the ball high and cross-court to the side wall about 3 feet short of the front-wall crotch, but not so high as to catch the ceiling. The ball will rebound off the front wall and then across to the other side wall just past mid-court (not as deep as the Z-ball). After hitting the second side wall, it should rebound directly at the other player on its way to the opposite rear corner. It's too high to hit offensively at that point, and also leaves very little left to hit in the back corner. The problem with the AWB is in hitting it high enough and deep enough without coming off the back wall for a setup.

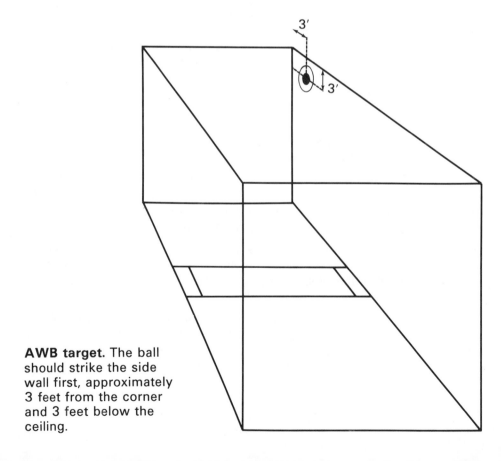

AWB target. The ball should strike the side wall first, approximately 3 feet from the corner and 3 feet below the ceiling.

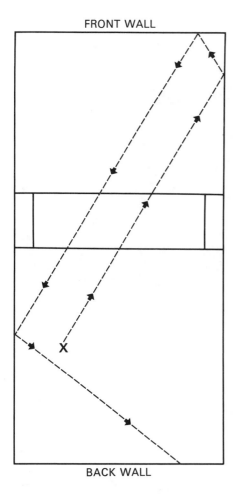

FRONT WALL

BACK WALL

Path of the AWB. The ball rebounds sharply off the side wall into the front wall, then carries diagonally into the back court and caroms off the second side wall with overspin toward the back wall.

Again, remember to get back into good position after striking the ball. Don't paint yourself into a corner with your own shot.

The AWB doesn't deserve an important niche in your defensive game. There are too many variables of height and angle to contend with. Too many setups as a result. The experienced, patient player can usually wait this one out and still have a good shot left. It might have some value in variety against a novice. But as a general rule, the ceiling shot is still your bread-and-butter for defense.

a

Reverse back-wall shot. Desperate to keep the ball in play after (a) a passing shot has eluded him, the player has only one choice: (b) to smash the ball into the back wall.

b

The Lob

The lob is a soft, high floater that's supposed to die in the back corner. It used to be the mainstay of defensive play. It was the very best way to force the opponent into the back court. When the live ball came in, the lob shot went out. The hopped-up rubber was just too difficult to control. Too many intended lobs rebounded off the back wall for easy setups. That's why the ceiling shot was developed. And that's why the lob shot is now virtually obsolete, except on the serve.

The Reverse Back-Wall Shot

As a shot goes past you on its way to the back wall, you have only two chances to stay alive. If it's high enough and hard enough to hit the back wall before the second bounce, you can chase it, get behind it, and hit a normal shot. But if it isn't going to make it that deep, your last resort is to smack it *into* the back wall with enough force to fly back to the front wall before the bounce—and that's the reverse back-wall shot. The result is still a weak shot, to be used only in desperation as a last-gasp point saver. It may accomplish no more than to keep you alive for one more shot, but then again, the other player might miss.

This shot is positively irresistible to the beginner. Its inherent contrariness lends an aura of romance to what is essentially a poor shot. The very idea of going south to get north! Imagine Pete Rose switching the bat to the other shoulder and hitting a single to centerfield—off the catcher? The images conjured up by this perversity are numerous.

Never hit this shot as a serve return just to avoid a difficult backhand. Never hit this shot if you can possibly get your racquet behind the ball to hit it forward. And a word on safety: Be aware of the possibility of getting hit by your own shot if you're too close to the back wall when you hit it. I've even seen players bleeding from their own racquets after bouncing the follow-through off the back wall into their faces. It's embarrassing. And it hurts.

Anticipation, movement, and position are all key elements in the tactics of racquetball. Here, the player in white moves quickly to the center-court area, where he will be able to control his opponent's return.

3

Strategy and Tactics

Strategy and tactics are what the book is all about. The first two sections were seduction and initiation; the last two will be development and expansion. This is the meat. This is about how to win.

Wanting to win just for the sake of winning is too often put down as being ruthless and bloodthirsty. Supposedly, winning has no intrinsic value of its own. But if winning is the direct result of deductive reasoning, planning, and physical preparedness—then it has value, both intellectually and spiritually. The joy of winning can be exquisite if it represents something above and beyond natural skills. If it is gained through dedication and perseverance, it is beautiful.

Racquetball is a microcosm of life—a learning environment which allows you to make mistakes without serious consequences. The challenges are to your intelligence, courage, and self-control. At the same time you undergo a test of the utilization of the full potential of your body. The satisfaction in using the raw materials of human anatomy to perform a physical act—begins very early in life. From the child learning to tie his shoe to the surgeon tying a similar knot with one hand, there's a thrill in it.

Winning must never be an obsession, but an ideal; not an ego trip, but an accomplishment; not a desire to crush an opponent, but rather a reaching out to attain new personal highs. Then it is not only moral but virtuous. To accept a challenge, to apply oneself to the maximum by analysis, effort, and conditioning, to use all of one's faculties—the brain as well as the body—thinking, then doing—that is the joy. Even the agony of defeat can have its own peculiar sweetness if dedication and commitment have been spent. If you give it your best shot, Rocky, you'll know that you're not just another bum from the neighborhood.

Enough philosophy. Now let's win this thing.

THE IMPORTANCE OF STRATEGY

Strategy counts for more in racquetball than in any other solo sport I know. Take bowling, for example. That is strictly a game of execution skills. A machine can bowl. If you can do it, great. If you can't, forget it. Golf is not far from bowling in that respect, a game of execution skills. I love the game, but it's not very interesting in a tactical sense. And in tennis, the player who can hit flawless ground strokes to the baseline isn't going to lose to any form of intelligence.

You can't hide your weaknesses in these sports; you can in racquetball. You can't select your opponent's shots in these sports; you can in racquetball. Imagine forcing your golf opponent to drive with his putter; in the figurative sense, you can do this in racquetball. Imagine hitting *his* ball behind a tree and forcing *him* to hit the next one; you can do this in racquetball. You can be a devious, shrewd, scheming puppeteer, manipulating the other player to your heart's desire. And then when you're quite ready, deliver the coup de grace in a variety of delicious ways. And that's what I call a pleasant way to spend an hour with a friend. Intriguing to the end. *If* you understand.

Racquetball is a great equalizer. Women can beat men, old can beat young, pygmies can beat giants. *If* they understand. You can't be overpowered, and there isn't very far to run. Size and strength have taken over in so many sports, it's refreshing to find one that pays off on skill and smartness. You can't beat a golfer who can drive and putt better than you, because you can't stop him from doing what he's good at. But you can beat a racquetball player who can hit kill shots with 100 percent accuracy—by preventing him from hitting kill shots. One hundred percent of nuthin' is nuthin'.

The Basic Winning Strategy

The basic winning strategy is so simple—and so seldom understood—and even less often adhered to. It is this:

1. *Hit a dead winner whenever you get a good chance.*
2. *If you feel you can't hit a dead winner, hit a perfect defensive shot.*
3. *NEVER hit anything in between.*

Before every shot, you have a question to answer: Have you a chance to end the point with one shot? This usually means, Have you a setup for a kill shot or passing shot? If the answer is yes, what remains is to choose the best winner to hit, which will be discussed later in detail. But if the answer is no, then you must hit a shot that gives him the *least* opportunity to hit a kill or pass of his own. This usually means a ceiling shot to the left corner. To put it another way—if you can't win the point immediately, try to guarantee yourself at least one more shot. Train yourself to be a four-wall schizophrenic—a cautious Dr. Jekyll when you don't have a good winning shot, a slashing Mr. Hyde when you do.

When I learned to play the guitar, I was told that if I mastered three chords, I could play 2,000 songs. I submit to you that if you could learn to hit three shots—the kill shot to the near corner, the cross-court pass, and the ceiling shot to the left corner—with reasonable accuracy and *at the right time,* you would win 95 percent of your racquetball games without hitting another shot. The shoulder-high, slam-the-ball-with-no-purpose, in-between half shots are the difference between the mediocre and the good racquetball player.

Action and Reaction

Strategy cannot be planned with rigidity. Racquetball is an "action-reaction" sport in every sense of the word. A general plan based on winning principles can be adhered to, that is true. But you cannot plan more than one shot ahead, because the next shot will be determined by the other player's position and return. There is no way to know in advance *where* you will be hitting your next shot from, and *where* he will be at the time. Your choice of shot will depend on those two factors.

A common misconception about chess is that the player plans many moves ahead, and then proceeds to execute his plan. This is not actually the case. The chess player maneuvers with only a loose, *general* plan in mind, but this plan is founded on many contingencies. He has prepared many variations to branch off from the original. On any given reply, he must change his plan and proceed with an alternate sequence of moves.

So it is with racquetball. Once you truly understand the principles, your opponent will virtually choose your shot for you. His position will tell you what to do.

The player with better kill shots and passing shots always wins? Hardly. The outcome must also depend on *how many* chances each player has. Let's say, for example, your opponent has 75 percent accuracy on kill-shot attempts, and you have only 50 percent. You can still beat him if your defensive play gives you more kill-shot chances. He might hit a lot of rollouts in practice, but a smart opponent will not permit him to take the shots in a match. The fact that players strike the ball in alternating turns gives the impression to the uninformed that both have an equal number of scoring chances. This is the grand illusion. What counts is not the number of strokes, but the number of chances to hit a *winner.* Count those at the end of a match and you'll find the totals quite unequal in favor of the victor.

In basketball, the team shooting layups will always beat the outside shooters, even though they might end up with the same number of shots at the hoop. The layup is shot from right under the basket. In racquetball our "layup area" is center court.

Center-Court Control

The principle of center-court control is often misunderstood. In a nutshell, what it means is this: If you can hit your shots from the short-line area, while forcing your opponent to shoot his from the back court, you can't lose unless you're playing with Marty Hogan. Don't pick up the wrong meaning of "center"; it doesn't mean halfway between the side walls. Many times it is correct to take a position to the right or left. It is the front-to-back axis, not the side-to-side axis, that is being referred to. You strive for a position halfway between the front and back walls—keeping your opponent *behind* you. That's what's meant by control.

Your success will ride heavily on the ratio of shots each player hits from the center-court area versus the back-court area. Only a monumental mismatch

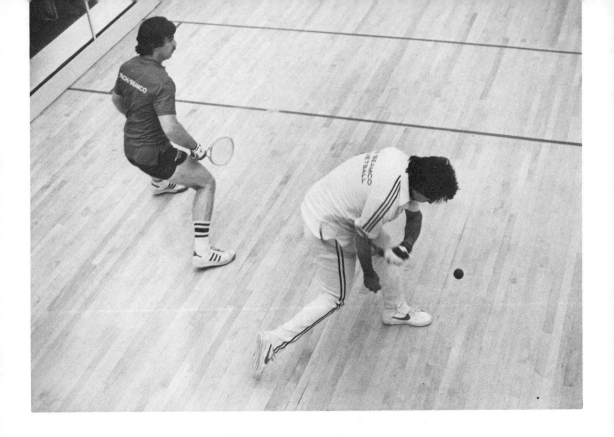

Center-court control is a must for winning points in racquetball. In the photo above, the player in black has been caught too far back and to the left, where he is vulnerable to a backhand passing shot down the right wall. In the photo at left, the player in white has established perfect position just behind the short line, where he can handle almost any shot his opponent can deliver.

would allow a player hitting all his shots from the back court to win. Most of the time, your shot should be followed by a move to an area one step behind the short line. When you are not trying to hit a winner, your objective should be to prevent the other player from getting a shot in this area. Force him to shoot from near the back wall, while you retain the prime court position.

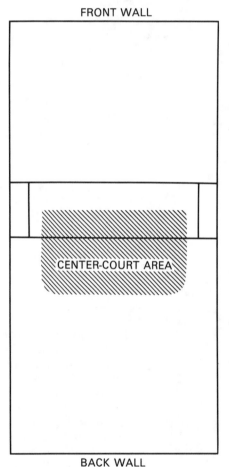

FRONT WALL

CENTER-COURT AREA

BACK WALL

Center-court area—the area of the court where most points are scored —where you should be thinking, "OFFENSE"

Pro Jerry Hilecher showing the serving form that earned him recognition as the best server in the game

THE SERVE

To define the object of the serve is to redefine the basic winning strategy: Either serve an ace or be sure you don't give the other player a setup on the return. If you don't go for an ace, try to make his shot as difficult as possible, in order to increase your chances for a winner on the second shot.

The service ace plays a prominent part in the tennis offense. It plays no part in badminton. In racquetball, it falls somewhere in between. It has more of a role at the pro level and less among amateurs. The average player is not required to hit great serves—just to avoid hitting poor ones.

Variety is crucial. Never let your opponent get grooved on a serve that you repeat without variation. The variations are infinite. However, regardless of the total number of possible serves, all serves can be divided into three types:

The Drive Serve

The drive serve is hit with a basic forehand stroke, so you want to drop the ball ahead and to the right. Then take a full stride into the shot near the service line. Whether you go left or right, there are two major variations:

The Short-Corner Drive

"Short-corner drive" is a misnomer, of course. The target is the "corner" made by the short line and side wall. This serve is your best chance for an ace. Try to "crack it out" just barely over the short line. The trick lies in hitting it hard enough to make it over the short line, yet low enough to make it stay down

a

b

c

d

Serve. Fundamental forehand form is adhered to with the advantage of being able to place the ball. (a) Begin with a comfortable stance; (b) drop the ball softly toward the opposite front corner; (c) as the ball bounces up, begin your stride and weight shift; (d) as the ball descends, plant the front foot and move the lower body into the shot. (e) The ball will be hit after it drops below the knee, and (f) the stroke is finished with a full follow-through.

e

f

84

Short-corner drive. Drive the ball low and hard with your target the side-wall–floor crotch, just beyond the short line.

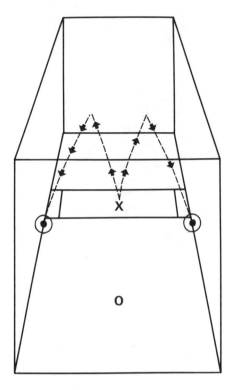

after the bounce. The timing, power, and wrist snap must be perfect. Variation is provided by changes in the server's position.

If you make an error on this one, you're better off to be short, so you'll have a chance to serve again. If you hit it too deep or too high, it will rebound off the side wall for a setup.

The Deep-Corner Drive

The deep-corner drive is the usual drive serve and the least risky. If you can keep this serve on a low trajectory, close to the floor, a ceiling shot is difficult to execute from it. Since a ceiling shot is the safest serve return, any serve that hampers it is a good serve. Many players will undercut the ball slightly, in order to make it stay low after the first bounce. The target is the back-corner crotch on the second bounce, and don't serve it too deep or it will rebound off the back wall for an easy return. Most pros will serve a deep-corner drive from a position slightly to the *left* of center. You may be called for a screen if the ball does not pass at least 18 inches from your body.

Develop a serving motion that allows you to go to either side with these serves without signaling the direction in advance. The short-corner drive to the *right* is always worth a few surprise points if you can hide your intent until contact.

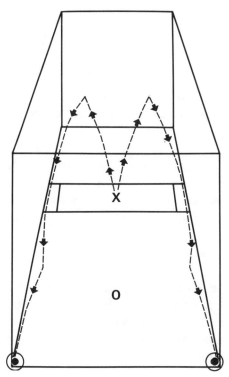

Deep-corner drive. Drive the ball low and hard toward the rear corner without touching the side wall—low enough to bounce twice before hitting the back wall.

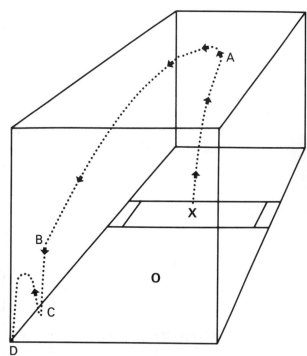

High lob serve. The ball is hit softly to a high, off-center point on the front wall (A); it floats lazily back to graze the side wall head-high (B), before hitting the floor (C), and dropping "dead" at the back wall (D).

The Lob Serve

The lob serve is a soft floater designed to force a shoulder-high return from back court. Easy to return but hard to return aggressively. There are three variations.

The High Lob Serve

The high lob serve is hit softly and high on the front wall so as to arch gently over the short line, graze the side wall head-high about 4 feet from the back wall, and drop dead in the corner. It takes the touch of a watchmaker to hit this one right. The margin for error is slim. If you can't hit it perfectly, don't hit it at all.

The Wallpaper Lob

For the wallpaper lob, take a position close to the side wall. Hit the ball, with either backhand or forehand, high on the front wall near the corner, so that it hugs the side wall throughout its entire course and dies in the back corner. There is an added risk here: If the ball touches the side wall *before* hitting the front wall, it is loss of serve without a second chance.

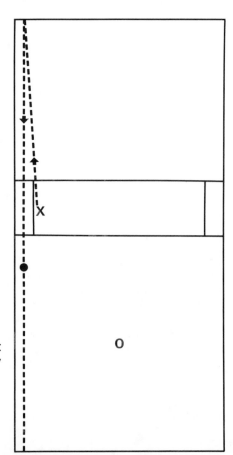

Wallpaper lob—a lob serve that hugs the side wall all the way

The Garbage Serve

The garbage serve is a half lob. The object is to hit a soft, shoulder-high floater a bit deeper without hitting the side wall. If hit to the proper depth, it leaves nothing but a shoulder-high back-court return. If controlled, this is a very effective serve to tame a kill-shot artist.

The Z-Serve

(The Z-serve is not to be confused with the Z-ball; on the serve the ball must strike the floor *before* it hits the third wall.) The concept of infinite variation on the serve applies more to this type than to the lob and drive serves. By subtle changes in the server's position, and in the angle, speed, height, and depth of the shot, you can come up with literally dozens of Z-serves, but few players take advantage of the full range of possibilities.

The basic Z-serve is struck from left of center to a spot on the front wall 2 feet from the right corner so as to rebound off the side wall and come back across court. It should bounce at three-quarter court depth, hit the side wall chest-high, and die in the back-wall crotch.

As for the many variations, some players, for instance, will bounce the ball high and hit an overhead; some will hit it underhand and high on the front wall to combine it with a lob effect. And, of course, you can go to either side with all variations. Here are a couple:

Variation 1

Deliver variation 1 from closer to the left wall. Hit the shot lower and more sharply into the corner, so it will come back at an acute angle to a more shallow position. This serve will resemble the "action" of a standard Z-ball jumping crazily cross-court after hitting the floor and second side wall.

Variation 2

My favorite variation is to deliver the serve from the *right* of center into the right front corner, where it bounds diagonally back to the left. You can vary the angle so as to hit the second side wall after the bounce one time and the back wall the next. This will give rise to an unsettling mixture of spins. If it hits the back wall after the bounce, it will usually surprise the other player by rebounding straight forward, rather than toward the side wall.

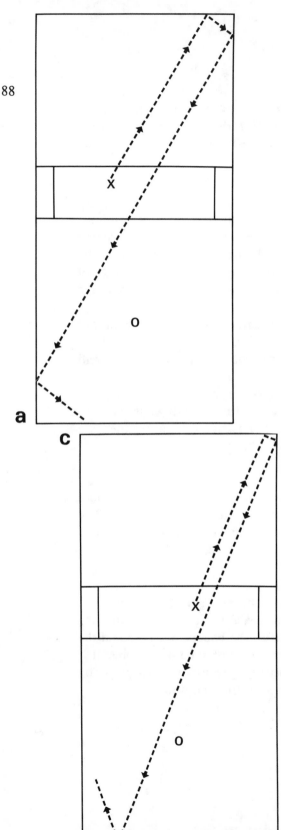

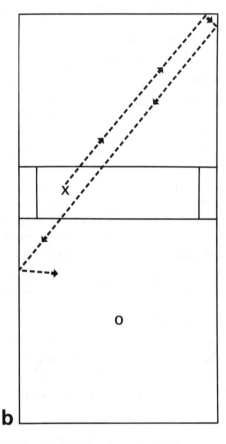

The Z-serve offers an unlimited number of variations, depending on the position of the server and the front-wall target. (a) Standard Z-serve, medium height and speed; (b) variation: hit lower and more sharply with more acute angling; (c) another variation. Key: to make contact with the ball to the *right* of center

Second Serves

To double-fault in racquetball is an unforgivable sin, because the legal target is very large and there's no net in the way as in tennis. But if your first serve goes astray, you must rearrange your priorities. Don't try for an ace with your second serve. You want something that is safe and reliable and has a wide margin for error without being a setup. The medium-hard Z-serve to the backhand corner serves all these purposes. Don't be careless. Too many second-serve setups are served up too casually and without thought.

After Serving

The moves the server makes after serving lead to some of the most common tactical errors in the game. It is best to discuss this subject by reviewing what *not* to do:

1. *Don't* take your eye off the ball. The identity badge of the novice is revealed by his backside as he turns his back on the ball and plants himself like an oak tree in center court. He has no idea where the next shot is going. He sacrifices half a step of mobility by failing to watch the position and body language of the other player. (Paul Haber, the great handball champion, says he never takes his eye off the ball—even during time-outs!)

2. *Don't* fade back like a quarterback. One step behind the short line is far enough. If you fade back farther, you're going to be embarrassed by mediocre kill shots that you can't get up to. It's hard to reverse your direction when you are backpedaling.

3. *Don't* drift (or stay) to the side opposite the ball. This makes you vulnerable to the down-the-wall pass.

4. *Don't* take a position midway between the side walls. One step over, in the direction of the ball, is correct. This not only gives you an edge in retrieving the down-the-wall kill-shot return, but it puts your body in the line of flight of a cross-court pass—and it's legal. The only lane you must leave open is the straight shot to the front wall.

a

Position after serving. After hitting
a Z-serve to the left corner (a), the
server quickly slides over to a better

b

position behind the short line just to
the left of center (b) and keeps his
eye on the ball.

General Comments on Serving

1. Concentrate. Don't just bang the ball into play. You have 10 seconds to serve. Use the time. Plan the serve. Plan your next move. Plan your response to the most likely return. No serve should be too casual.

2. Be sure to develop a right-side serving game, to augment the usual serves to the backhand corner. Weakness against the Z-serve to the right corner is surprisingly common, even among good forehand shooters. The pros make good use of this weapon, often neglected by the novice.

3. Be ready to compensate for your serving errors. If your Z-serve is coming in too shallow, look out for the cross-court pass—move over and back a step. If your drive serve is slightly too deep and comes up on the back wall, look out for the down-the-wall kill shot—move up a step.

4. Always test out your opponent with a wide variety of serves early in the game. You might discover a glaring weakness, and you can "go back to the well" when you need to most.

5. Take the most offensive chances on your second shot. You have him more out of position than you may ever have again. Be aggressive. Go for the winner even if you don't have a perfect setup. You should hit more fly kills after the serve return than at any other time.

THE SERVE RETURN

The serve return is the most important shot in the game. Back up and read that again—and again. And believe. If you're looking for a part of the game to begin your uphill climb, this is it.

Statistical studies reveal that as many as 50 percent of all the points scored in racquetball are scored on the *second shot*. It's not so surprising, after all, when you begin to analyze the reasons:

The server begins with the best position on the court; you have the worst.

The server hits any serve he desires; you are forced into a position of *his* choice.

The server knows where the serve is going; you don't.

There's more pressure on you because you lose a point for an error; he doesn't.

Watch a few matches with this in mind. Take note of how many points are scored as a result of weak serve returns that lead to a setup kill or pass shot by the server. The player who is behind is invariably the one returning serve poorly. Before moving on to specific stratagems, a few basic rules should be set down:

1. Don't play too far back. Many players take a position only one step out from the back wall to receive serve, becoming highly vulnerable to the short-corner drive serve. Protect yourself by moving up almost halfway to the short line. You'll have plenty of time to get back for the deep serve, if necessary.

2. Never decide on your return before you see the serve. Your chances for good execution are drastically affected by the depth, angle, height, and speed of the ball. Let these factors determine your shot selection. It may be fatal to choose your shot in advance.

"The serve return is the most important shot. . . . If you're looking for a part of the game to begin your uphill climb, this is it."

---

3. Always be ready to abandon the "normal" shot if the server moves out of position. Punish the "faders" and the "drifters." If the server fades back more than a step, he has an unrealistic phobia about being passed. Grant him his wish. Don't pass him. Exterminate him with a kill-shot return. It doesn't even have to be a very good one. A player in reverse has a tough time shifting gears to reach even a poor kill shot.

Punish the drifter who errs by moving laterally *away* from the ball. Burn him with a down-the-wall pass.

4. Move up and hit the lob serve before the bounce whenever you can —unless it's obviously going to be deep enough for a back-wall setup. A good lob-serve touch artist can give you a bad case of the screaming meemies if you don't move up. The soft, high Z-serves are also best hit on the fly.

5. Mobility is important. Don't be flat-footed. Start your pivot early and get your body into a hitting position.

6. Always follow your shot with a move up into a better position. Don't freeze in your tracks admiring your shot.

The Object of the Serve Return

If you can prevent the server from scoring on his second shot, you have an even chance to win the exchange. There are two ways of doing this. Either end the point with one shot, or force him into a bad position to prevent him from ending it with the next one. Against the majority of serves, the latter is the sensible choice. The best way to accomplish it is with a ceiling shot to the left corner.

The Ceiling-Shot Return

The mainstay of your serve-return game should be the ceiling-shot return. It gives you the best chance of forcing the server into the back court. Against poor serves, you may be more aggressive with kills and passes. But a good player won't set up many pumpkins for you to shoot at. The burden is transferred to you to prevent him from having the setup on the next shot. A good ceiling shot to the left corner will force him to hit a chest-high backhand scrape off the side wall. He will usually return another ceiling shot, but even this may be difficult to place if he is driven well back into the corner.

A consistent tight ceiling shot to the left corner will save you more points in the long run than any other shot in the game.

The Kill-Shot Return

The kill-shot return is the quickest way to get the serve back—also the most dangerous. If it's hit too low, it skips in for a loser. If it's too high, the server has you at his mercy and can beat you several ways. The shot must be executed with even more precision than most kill shots because you are catering to a positional advantage. Your position is the very worst, while his, if he pays attention, is the very best. Your margin of error is very slim. Either bury it low into the corner, or you'd better hit a different shot. Choose your spots well and always go down-the-wall to the near corner. A cross-court kill against the serve is a poor percentage shot. Save it for mid-court setups. For most players the kill-shot return should be reserved for three situations:

> The serve setup is irresistibly poor.
> The server fades to the back door.
> You're too tired to hit more than one shot.

The Cross-Court-Pass Return

This shot can be used for both offensive and defensive purposes:

Offensive—try this shot for a winner primarily in two situations, for the serve that comes in shallow, and for punishing the server who has his back turned.

Defensive—the only viable substitute for a poor ceiling game. Until you get that ceiling shot whipped into shape, rely on the cross-court drive to keep the server at bay. The disadvantage, when compared to the ceiling shot, is that you usually feed his forehand.

The above three shots should account for 95 percent of your serve returns.

Less Important Serve Returns

Down-the-Wall Pass—should be used only in response to the drift, the lateral move error away from the ball.

Cross-Court Kill—not wise on serve return.

Ceiling Shot to the Right Corner—a good choice in response to a surprise low drive serve to the right, one that you can barely reach.

Around-the-Wall Ball (AWB)—all right to mix in with your ceiling shots, but harder to control.

Z-Ball—seldom called for on serve return. Most serves coming in shallow enough to allow for a Z-ball attempt should be answered with a kill shot or cross-court pass. The exception might be the high lob that you move up on to hit on the fly.

Lob—not with the new live ball, you don't.

WINNING THE POINT—THE RALLY

Shot selection isn't a science. It's an art. Understanding the basic winning strategy is fine, but to make it work, you must prove it with an intelligent choice of shots. It's not enough to know that your shots should be restricted to dead winners or perfect defensive shots. With every shot there is only an instant to decide which of the two is called for—and then to choose the exact response that fits. The great players react instinctively. Your eventual goal is the same, but you must begin by using an analytical approach.

Your decision to opt for an offensive or defensive shot should depend on three factors:

Your Court Position

Generally, the closer you are to the front wall, the better chance you have to hit a winner. When you find yourself hitting from deeper than three-quarter court, you are usually obligated to hit a defensive shot.

Opponent's Court Position

The above applies to any situation that finds your opponent in the correct position. If he isn't where he should be, your choice should be changed accordingly.

The Height of the Ball

Ball height at contact must also be considered. As discussed in the fundamentals section, kill shots should be hit at ankle height, passing shots at knee height. Even when you're in perfect position, it's tough to hit a kill shot on a ball in front of your nose.

Let's apply these factors to actual situations and determine their relative values in each:

Example. You have a knee-high setup near the short line. This calls for a shot at a winner no matter where your opponent is. His position will help you choose between the kill shot or pass.

Example. You're faced with a shoulder-high ceiling shot down the middle in back court. Normally, the height of the ball and your court position would dictate a defensive shot. Throw that reasoning out the window if you see your opponent lagging in back court. Go for the overhead kill. In this example, his court position is the most important factor.

Example. You serve to the left corner. Your opponent tries a cross-court pass that fails. It comes back to your forehand waist high. Kill shots are normally hit from below the knee, but make an exception here because of his backward position and your prime position. Cut the ball off and go for the fly kill to the near corner.

Example. Your opponent hits a perfect ceiling shot which crawls along the left wall, shoulder high in back court. You must return a defensive shot, even if he is out of position. Your poor position and the height of the ball combine to overrule his position disadvantage.

Throughout the game, you will be trying to provoke a weak return so that you have a chance to go for a winner. When you succeed in getting that chance, you must take it. No matter how strong your ceiling game is, you can't just stand there hitting ceiling shots all day, waiting for him to miss. You can't depend on your opponent to self-destruct. You have to beat him to win. If you don't jump all over that setup, the next one might be his. Decide quickly on a shot—and hit it. Don't be tentative.

Naturally, the same applies to backhand chances. Many players consider themselves quite accomplished on the left side when they develop a good backhand defensive game. They have good form, and they hit good ceiling shots. But they never *score* with their backhand. The sad truth is that there are many more scoring chances on the left side than on the right, because most players bombard the opponent's backhand. Yet when you count the winners at the end of the day, most have been hit with the forehand. How can this be? The answer is that the majority of players don't take the kill shot when it's set up on the left. They cop out with the cross-court pass, which will never work if the other player knows it's coming.

The Point Winners

There are two basic winners in racquetball—the kill shot and the passing shot.

There are two basic strokes in racquetball—the forehand and the backhand.

There are two sides to a racquetball court—the right and the left.

Add up all the possibilities and we arrive at eight winning shots in racquetball:

1. Forehand kill shot to the right corner
2. Forehand kill shot to the left corner
3. Forehand passing shot down the right side
4. Forehand passing shot down the left side
5. Backhand kill shot to the left corner
6. Backhand kill shot to the right corner
7. Backhand passing shot down the left side
8. Backhand passing shot down the right side

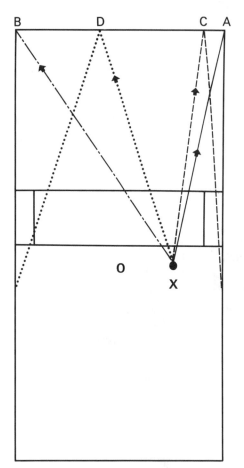

Forehand winners. On a right-side offensive setup, the shooter must choose the best of four possible "winners" on the basis of the opponent's position: (A) near-corner kill shot; (B) cross-court kill shot; (C) down-the-wall pass; (D) cross-court pass.

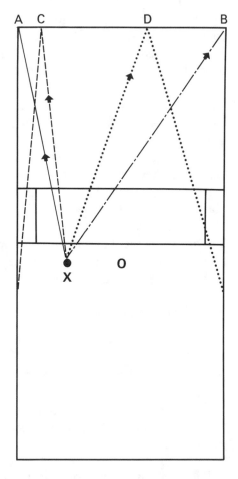

Backhand winners. On a left-side offensive setup, the shooter must choose the best of four possible "winners" on the basis of the opponent's position: (A) near-corner kill shot; (B) cross-court kill shot; (C) down-the-wall pass; (D) cross-court pass.

These eight shots make up your offensive attack. All eight are important. You won't hit them in equal numbers, but there will always be certain setups where you have a chance to score with only one shot out of the eight. When you practice, deal with each one as a separate entity. Don't make the mistake of assuming that a good forehand kill to the right corner guarantees you the ability to be just as accurate to the left. It's a different shot. The feet alignment and pivot put you in a different position. Practice it.

The greatest challenge to most players is to develop a backhand that can be hit with the same confidence they have in their forehand kill shot. Until you reach that summit, you have only half an offense.

The Double Threat

A setup is a setup because you are in a position to threaten *two* things which cannot be defended by *one* player. This principle is the essence of the offense in most games. Basketball has its two-on-one fast break; football its pass-run option play; chess its knight fork. It even applies in tic-tac-toe. They all operate on the strength of the double threat.

In racquetball the double threat is provided by the marriage of the near-side kill shot and the cross-court pass. On a right-side setup near the short line, you threaten the kill shot to the right corner. If your opponent moves up, you simply pass him on the left. If he guesses the same shot on the next setup, and lays back for the pass—you bury the kill shot into the right corner. And so it goes throughout the game. But you must have all the shots in your bag, or the threat is full of blanks and is certain to be recognized as such by a smart player.

Double-threat setup. The defender has little chance—he cannot simultaneously defend the near-corner kill (A) and the cross-court pass (B).

The kill shot is seen here from the inevitable end point of its floor-hugging journey—the right front corner. (Jerry Hilecher)

Kill Shots

Your target should be the corner. The height of the target is usually 6–12 inches but will vary with the position of the other player. If he is stranded in back court, there is no need to risk going for bottom board. Naturally, if you miss the target, you're better off missing on the high side. Keep the ball in play and you're still alive. The low skip-in ends the point.

The straight-out kill is a higher-percentage shot than the pinch. The latter "pinches" the corner by hitting the side wall and front wall before the floor. It adds another dimension by adding a second wall, reducing the margin for error. Never try to hit a wide-angled pinch shot. This would lower the odds even more. Always keep your pinch shots within 3 feet of the corner.

Go for the *near* corner 90 percent of the time. For one thing, that's the closer target. Second, you have the visual advantage of the side wall as a parallel guide line for your shot. The best time to try a cross-court kill shot is on a ball angling toward you *from* the target area. It's not too difficult to line yourself up and return the ball down the same line of flight. It's far more difficult to divert the line of flight 90 degrees on a ball coming from the other corner.

Don't give up on the kill shot if you miss a few early in a match. When the shot is there, it must be hit. A common mistake is to cut down on the power and try to guide the ball after a few misses. The opposite will work better. Hit it *harder.* You will be able to hold your shooting line better with firmness than with finesse.

Passing Shots

The passing shot is the safer of the two offensive weapons. The penalty for missing a kill shot, either high or low, is usually loss of point. If you mishit a passing shot, you still have a fighting chance to stay in the hunt. For this reason, it's best for beginners—and even for most intermediate players—to rely on an offense that emphasizes passing shots.

The choices of left versus right, and V-pass versus down-the-wall pass, are dictated by the position of the other player. But the "obvious" is not always the best shot. A player who is caught on the left side is charging so hard back to the center that he can often be beaten more easily by a pass back to the left. His momentum is hard to reverse.

Remember that the most common passing-shot error is hitting the ball too high on the front wall. No matter how perfect the angle of the pass, it's worthless if it rebounds off the back wall. Your target should be 2–3 feet high on the front wall.

As for angle, if it's not a perfect pass, it's better to be too wide than not wide enough. The shot that rebounds off the side wall right at the other player is harder to handle than one coming straight back from the front wall. The latter provides too many fly-kill setups that give you no chance.

Finally, always move back toward the center after hitting a cross-court passing shot. If the other player intercepts the pass, you won't be so vulnerable to the quick pop to the near corner.

The Fly Shot

The fly shot, also known as the cut-off shot and the volley, is hit before the bounce. Many good winning chances are lost by letting the ball bounce first and retrieving it off the back wall. Learn to execute kill shots and passing shots on the fly, plucked out of the air waist high—to use when your opponent is out of position. Your accuracy won't be quite as good, but will be more than compensated for by the positional plus. Why give him time to move up into prime position? Why choose to hit your shot from back court when you could be hitting from the short-line area?

Marty Hogan feels that the ability to execute the fly kill with consistency is one of the major steps toward becoming a Class A racquetball player.

The Drop Shot

The drop shot is a touch shot, delivered as a soft tap to a low point on the front wall, usually near the corner. It is designed to drop quickly, to be impossible to retrieve before the second bounce. It used to enjoy a more prominent, and well-deserved, place in the offense during the old dead-ball days. Now you cannot get away with this shot unless you are within two steps of the front wall. To execute properly, you must wait for the drop. Never try this shot from above the knee. Two situations make the drop shot a winning option:

1. When your opponent tries a kill shot that you can barely get to, a quick drop shot to the near corner can give you the winner. Anything else you might try from such a forward position will usually be answered with a passing shot zinging right by your ear.

2. When your opponent misses the ceiling, the ball will rebound off the back wall with force and carry far into front court. If it drops below the knee, the drop shot is a good choice against the player who lays back. (If the ball is above the knee as it drives you close to the front wall, you're better off going to the ceiling and trying to regroup. This ceiling shot is hit in reverse—front wall first—which would become painfully obvious the first time you tried it the usual way. If you try to hit the ceiling first from front court, the ball is likely to come straight down on top of your head.)

Drop shot. The shooter catches his opponent in the back court and taps the ball softly into the corner.

The most common error in executing the drop shot is hitting it too high and too hard. Take into account the added force provided by your forward momentum as you charge toward the front wall. Just tap the ball, with little or no wrist action. And always disguise the shot until the last instant, with the threat of a cross-court pass lurking in the wings. That keeps your opponent from following you in.

What's the error? Good form but poor court position for a drop shot. The player should be well up ahead of the service line to have any hope of succeeding with this shot.

The Overhead Kill Shot

The beauty of a well-placed ceiling shot is that it allows no good choice on the return other than another ceiling shot. This can lead to long dull exchange rallies. If your opponent is lulled to sleep by the repetition and fails to get back into position near the short line, you have a chance to destroy him with an overhead kill shot. Generally, this is possible with the forehand only; the backhand overhead is too hard to control. But you must never try this shot against the player who gets back to prime position.

You can go to either corner, but it is usually best to go cross-court, hitting the side wall first as a pinch shot. You won't be able to hit it quite as low as the normal kill shot, but you don't have to. Your yawning opponent will be fixated in the rear corner where he received your last umpteen shots—looking up at the ceiling, wondering where the ball went. Hide your intention until the last instant.

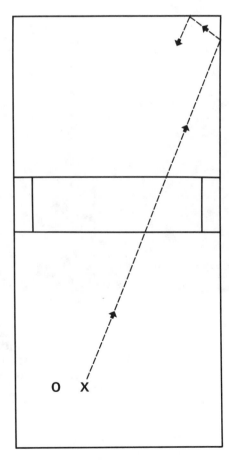

Overhead kill shot. This low-percentage shot is chosen only when the other player is badly out of position.

a **b**

Position in ceiling-shot exchange. To guard against the overhead kill you must get back into good position after *every* ceiling shot: (a) the player is about to return a ceiling shot; (b) the ball is on its way to the target; (c) the player quickly moves up; (d) now in prime position, with his eye on the ball, he is no longer vulnerable.

Body Language

If you heed the dictum on ball watching, your eye will eventually be led back to the other player. Then it's time to transfer your attention briefly from the ball to him. Observe his motion closely. You might pick up a clue as to whether he will hit a kill shot or a pass. A half-step-early move can bail you out of an otherwise losing position. We're talking about fractions of a second, but that can make the difference in getting to the ball. There are five tip-offs that might signal a kill shot rather than a pass:

1. More wrist cock
2. Longer backswing
3. Longer stride into the shot
4. Knees bent lower
5. Lower point of contact

As every player is different, these tip-offs are not guaranteed; you should be aware of your opponent's peculiarities of style as you watch for clues to his shots.

Such body language may be of limited value in a setup situation, but can definitely be helpful in anticipating an opponent who has his back to you, hitting an errant ceiling shot that's about to come off the back wall. You can slip up ahead of the short line and gobble up his "winner." There are few things more gratifying than to make a sensational get by reading his shot before he hits it. How sweet it is! And how equally demoralizing for the opponent. He has hit a good kill shot only to watch it being rekilled by a smarter player who had the jump on it. That's like stroking a great putt and looking up to find that the hole has been filled in.

Always try to soak up every bit of advance information you can during the course of play. It may be worth a point or two. And that might be just the difference between winning and losing.

"There are few things more gratifying than to make a sensational get by reading your opponent's shot before he hits it."

The Setup (When It's His)

Don't give up when you've hit a bad shot and he's about to deliver his favorite forehand kill. As long as the ball is in play, you still have a chance. There is only one thing to do:

Take away his best shot.

The instant before he hits the ball, make an early move toward the target corner. Show yourself to him. Force him to try to make a perfect shot—or change it. Admittedly, you take yourself out of position by the early move, but you have nothing to lose. You might just intimidate him into taking his eye off the ball and hitting it into the floor. You won't reach the rollout, but you might get to the one that comes up a little high. Naturally, his best reaction is to change his shot and hit a cross-court pass. If it's too high, you get another chance off the back wall. In any case, this move will at least give you some chance where you had none. Try it. It's better than just standing there at the gallows waiting to die. Make a run for it. Or at least fake a move.

VARIATIONS IN STRATEGY

It has been stressed and restressed in these pages that racquetball is an action-reaction game. Golfers are coached to "play the golf course, not the other player." That won't do in racquetball. If you bullheadedly plow ahead with a rigid, unyielding approach to this game, you're going to get blitzed. You cannot ignore what your opponent is doing. If you are unable or unwilling to adapt your game to fit the other player's weakness, you are going to find yourself losing to people with less ability. Every move you make, every shot you hit, should be calculated to cancel out his strength and exaggerate yours; to illustrate his weakness and cover up yours. Matters of style, speed, shooting ability, and fitness must all be taken into account. Then you mold your game to fit the needs.

Let's analyze a few different strategies.

How to Kill a Killer

You all know Killer. He's Babe Ruth, Rocky Marciano, and Pistol Pete Maravich all wrapped up into one. Always trying to beat you with one shot. On *every* shot. He walks onto the court with monovision—kill shots, kill shots, and more kill shots. If he's a terrible shooter and keeps on slamming the ball into the floor, you can laugh your way to victory over the masochist. But if he can roll them out with consistency, you have a formidable problem to cope with. What should you do?

Shoot more; i.e., go for more winners.

The usual response to this line of thought is, "That would be playing *his* game." Nonsense. You won't be playing his game at all. You'll be *taking away* his game.

Don't play the waiting game with Killer. You might be capable of hitting perfect ceiling shots 90 percent of the time, but eventually you'll hit a weak one. Don't be blind to the inevitable. Sooner or later he will get his shot and it's lights out. Try to hit as many *early* winners as possible. Give him fewer chances to exercise his strength. You must take more aggressive chances against this player. Expand the usual criteria for offensive play. Hit more kill shots on serve return. When you can, stop him from scoring before he has even one chance to shoot the ball. He can't *serve* a kill shot.

The same strategy applies if you're up against a better player. The longer the point goes on, the more likely he is to win it. You wouldn't dispute the fact that the underdog has a better chance to win a 5-point game than a full one. Doesn't the same reasoning apply to the individual rally? So why not shoot more?

A couple of years ago I played an exhibition against a pro. Two-time national champ Bill Schmidtke was in town giving a clinic. Understand now: A tactician I am; a writer I'm trying to be; a gifted athlete I'm not. I knew my chances were somewhere between failure and death. I had three choices—leave town, call in sick with the palsy, or go out onto the court and SHOOT everything I could get my racquet on. I chose the third, of course, and managed to get 13 points—about 10 more than I would have gotten with my usual methodical, waiting game.

The next time you come up head to head with Killer, or draw the number-one seed in a tournament, remember this: there is only one sure way to keep him from hitting a kill shot—and that is to keep him from hitting *any* shot. End the point.

How to Catch a Rabbit

You all know this guy, too. Charlie Hustle. Great agility and quick reflexes. The speed demon, the racehorse. He makes Pete Rose look like he's doggin' it. Charging around the court, diving, crashing into walls, but always hitting your best shot back. You need 63 winners to get 21 points against this guy. You have to "beat" him three times for every score. 111

But he isn't a topnotch shooter like Killer. (If he is, find someone else to play with.) He is basically a retriever; an All-American shot-catcher. If you try to play the shooting game, you show off *his* talents. Half your kill shots he will miraculously save, and the other half you'll hit into the floor, trying to hit it lower and lower.

Apply the same principle as we did to Killer. Take away his strength. Play a game that gives no prizes for speed. Slow down the tempo. This means lofting a series of left-corner ceiling shots at him, with a few Z-balls mixed in for variety. Hit winners only when he makes the inevitable weak return that allows you to annihilate him three ways. It makes no sense to take high-risk gambling shots against a good fast Rabbit.

This strategy turns a winning Rabbit into a nervous Rabbit. It will eventually frustrate him so much that he is likely to make some bad shots. He'll stoop to anything to halt the ceiling-shot exchange and restore *his* kind of pace. And that's when he gives you the game.

How to catch a Rabbit? Just bore him to death.

Winning Tired

(Or, how to shoot when you're shot; or, how to start when you're finished; or, how to do when you're done.)

Choose your own label, but I know many of you are afflicted with the Spear Syndrome: over forty, legs starting to give out (to say nothing of the lungs), endurance on the wane, speed no more than a distant memory. What adds to the malignancy is the depressing contrast in the youthful adversary, the prancing gazelle. With no compassion, he stays on the court to play another hour as we stagger off to the intensive care unit, clutching a picture of George Blanda to our hearts.

Watch for the warning signals. Are your nailbeds turning purple? Have you stopped sweating on one half of your body? Do you see palm trees and watery oases in front court? Take heart. All is not lost. Simply unveil Plan B, and you might still pull through.

1. Concentrate. Mental mistakes multiply with the onset of fatigue. Your "thinking" game will suffer more than your running or shooting game.

2. When serving, be careful not to set up any pumpkins. It isn't necessary to make great serves. Just avoid hitting poor ones.

3. When returning serve, hit a kill shot every good chance you have.

Keep the rally as short as possible. Shotmaking skills deteriorate with exhaustion. You have the most energy early in the point, so set yourself up and go for the winner. The longer the rally goes on, the more likely you are to make an error.

4. Play aggressively. Go for every point. Don't make the mistake of trying to pace yourself, saving something for the later stages. If you don't win some points, you'll never see the later stages. Try to make the game as short as possible and you have a chance.

5. In shotmaking, concentrate on lower-body action. The first flaw to appear in a tired player is the backhand shot hit from a face-front, flat-footed position—no pivot. You won't get away with it. Always make your full turn and stride into the shot.

6. Take the full ten seconds allotted to you by the rules between every point. Before you serve, just hold the ball and inhale the oxygen. If you are receiving, just turn your back on the server (or hold up your hand), relax, breathe, and wait out the time.

Beating the Tired Player (Mercy Killing)

This subject is foreign to me. I feel remote. I've never been here before. It's like trying to describe a painting I've never seen. The tired player has always been *me.*

Just the same, it's only fair to analyze the situation from the point of view of the other player as well, painful as it may be. If the stamina of your opponent begins to deteriorate, consider the following:

1. When serving, stay with the low drive to both sides. Your opponent has much less time to react to a "no-wall" serve than to a Z-serve that hits three or four walls, or a lob that takes forever to get there.

2. On serve return, watch for him to fade back too far. The tired player often commits this error and should be punished with a kill-shot return. Don't try to roll it out. A medium—1-foot-high—kill shot will do. He'll never get there. (If he dosen't fade, don't hit kill-shot returns.)

3. Hit passing shots early in the rally, then shift gears and hit a kill shot. He will tend to play further back as the rally goes on.

4. Move the ball around. Standing in one spot trading ceiling shots with a foggy player throws away your advantage. Try more overhead kills when he lags back.

5. Dig extra hard on long rallies. Keep the ball in play. Every shot you

can add to the exchange raises the odds he'll make an error on the next one.

6. Try an occasional hard, low drive that rebounds right at him. This presents more of a challenge than it seems. It requires a nimble reset of feet and body position. The pooped-out player doesn't handle that well.

7. Play good solid racquetball. Don't be tempted to throw away all your well-disciplined principles of strategy just because your opponent is drained. You can't just pop the ball around and expect him to miss everything. Don't lose your total perspective; all these suggestions are merely adjuncts to the fundamental strategy, which should never be abandoned.

Psyching Your Way to Glory

The mental game. Anything you can do, ethically of course, to break the spirit or disturb the concentration of the other player is worth a few points. Charlie Brumfield has been winning that way for years. It's not immoral. It's not illegal. It's all part of the game. Here are a few ideas:

1. Pause during the pregame warmup and watch your opponent's feet. It may bother him some, wondering what his motion is revealing. (Remember the old golf psych, "Do you inhale or exhale on your backswing?") At the same time, you might pick up a few tips on his body language.

2. If you lose the coin flip, hit a kill shot on your opponent's first serve if you can. A player rarely expects this. If you succeed, you might rattle him. If not, it's only 1 point on the long road to 21.

3. If he serves a lob, charge it and hit it on the fly. This is unnerving to a lob server early in the game, and you immediately take charge of the tempo.

4. If you serve first, try for an ace with a low-drive, short-corner serve. He won't be ready for it. He'll still be checking to see if his socks are up straight. It's a great way to get off to a flying start.

5. Super-hustle on the first 3 or 4 points of the game. Don't pace yourself. Create the illusion that you are going after, and are capable of getting to, *absolutely everything.* This can shake your opponent's confidence in a bad way. It's also a good way to relieve tension.

6. Put out your biggest effort on the long rallies. The longer the point goes on, the more you run. It's demoralizing for him to lose a point after he has played his heart out.

7. It's even worse to lose the serve on one shot after hitting fifteen or twenty to win the last one. So if you lose one of those marathon rallies, try killing the very next serve. It's a great morale-buster. Hogan does it all the time.

8. Call your time-outs when you gain some psychological advantage, not just to rest. Before serving match point in a close match, a time-out is worth a few shakes from your opponent's knees.

Strategy Tidbits

Here are a few unrelated, isolated tips which don't fall conveniently into any category. These should serve to round out the discussion of strategy and tactics in singles.

1. Watch for less alert players to get trapped on the left wall by their own Z-serves. If they don't slide over to prime position after serving, hit the pass down the right side.

2. The player who serves to the right corner tends to drift left of center. Beat him with a forehand down-the-wall pass.

3. If your kill shots are off, hit a few cross-court. The change in angle might help you find the range. Then you can return to the normal target.

4. When the opponent is trapped against one side wall by the flight of his own shot, don't rush your shot. Until you hit the ball, he can't move anyway without being called for an avoidable hinder.

5. The best way to break a losing streak is to run harder. It takes more effort to get fired up when you're feeling down.

6. Take the off-center position *any* time the shot is coming from the rear corner, not only after serving. The principles are the same.

7. If you run into a super-live ball, which is not rare nowadays, you might have trouble keeping your usual ceiling shot off of the back wall. Try a few front-wall-first ceiling shots. They won't carry quite as deep.

8. The average player stays back too far. If you "take pride" in never being passed, you've got nothing to be proud of—you're just playing back too far. If you don't lose nearly as many points on passes as kill shots, you're playing back too far. Most players could add 3–5 points to their scores tomorrow by playing 1–2 steps up for everything. So don't vegetate at three-quarter depth. Move up around the short line.

9. Don't play two different strategies based on whether you are serving or receiving. Some players peddle the "be more aggressive when serving, less aggressive when receiving" theory. Strictly Dumbsville. The principles of winning strategy apply equally to both situations. Shot selection should not be altered. Always play the right shot. The score will take care of itself.

10. When your opponent hits a reverse back-wall shot, move up into

front court and hit it on the fly, before he has a chance to get back up into position. A drop shot should do it, or a fly kill if you wish.

11. If your opponent waits to hit your ceiling shot until *after* it hits the back wall, a kill shot is more likely than a cross-court pass. Move up.

DOUBLES

There are many players who love the game of doubles; some even prefer it to singles. To those players I can only offer encouragement. By all means go ahead with the game that you enjoy the most. There are a few inherent advantages in doubles, such as the heightened "social" pleasure of having four players on the court to romp around with. And to the player who can't quite meet the physical demands of an hour of singles coverage, it might be said that half a court is better than none. But I don't want to gloss over my own personal prejudice against doubles. For the most part I see it as a perversion of a gorgeous sport—finesse transmuted into a brawl. The ultracerebral chess game becomes a chaos of four players seeming to throw the pieces at each other. Both tennis and handball allow for great doubles action without losing the intrinsic soul of the game. Racquetball doubles is not a natural extension of the singles game but a totally different game and, in my view, a poor one.

The Rules

Overall rules and scoring are the same. A few wrinkles are added regarding the serve. Each member of a team is allowed to continue serving until the exchange is lost. A "side-out" is called after both have lost the exchange. (The exception is on the very first serve of a game, when loss of *one* exchange is a side-out.) No restrictions are made on choice of direction in serving (as in tennis), or during the rally.

Court Coverage

Each team must decide on how to divide the court into areas of influence. Depending on the strengths and weaknesses of the players, the selection will usually be made from one of the three following systems:

Doubles court coverage.
(a) Side-by-side system;
(b) front-back system;
(c) diagonal system

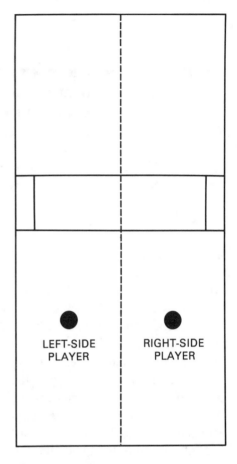

LEFT-SIDE
PLAYER

RIGHT-SIDE
PLAYER

a

Side-by-Side System

An imaginary line is drawn down the middle, running the entire length of the court (such as the one you have in mind when you decide whether to hit a forehand or backhand). Choice of sides should be determined on the basis of backhand strength, because that's where most of the action will be. The player with the stronger backhand plays the left side. If one partner is left-handed, he plays the left side so the team can cover both corners with forehand control.

Front-Back System

One player plays up near the short line, the other acts as a back-court rover, covering all deep shots. The speedier player should play up front so as to have a better chance to retrieve kill-shot attempts. The player with the stronger ceiling-shot game belongs in the back court.

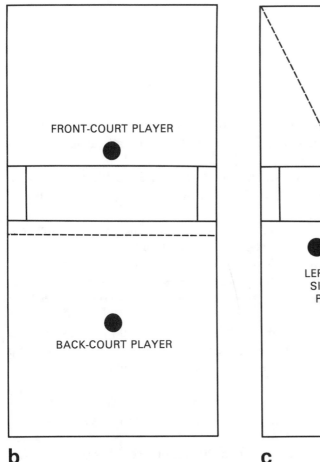

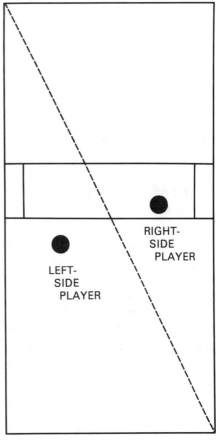

b   c

Diagonal System

An imaginary dividing line runs from the left front corner to the right rear corner. The player on the right covers most of the front court and the right back corner. The other player covers most of the back court and the left front corner. Once again the faster player should be on the right of the diagonal, and the player with the strong ceiling game on the left.

The side-by-side system is by far the most popular and most logical of the three. It is the least complicated to execute and will work out best for most doubles teams. There are a few teams that have refined the other systems to make them work. More often than not, this has been necessitated by a peculiarity in style or a vast difference in ability between the two partners.

Strategy

A few pointers:

1. Carve up the weaker player. (This is no time for social amenities.) This calls for a right-sided attack most of the time, in contrast to the usual backhand emphasis in singles.

2. Hit kill shots only on surefire setups near the short line. Otherwise, rely for offense on V-passes that jam the player with a ball coming right at him off the side wall.

3. To avoid being the victim of the latter ploy, take your position well *away* from the side wall—almost rubbing elbows with your partner.

4. Anticipate your partner's shot as well as the opponents' shots. If your partner's winning shot hits your body before the second bounce, you lose the point, and you'll be the target of a laser-beam stare such as you've never been hit with before.

5. On defense, the player on the "action" side should play up closer to the front wall. You can even risk being ahead of the short line to get the jump on a kill shot. The cross-court pass isn't a threat as it is in singles. It's being covered by your partner.

6. Don't be impatient during long ceiling-shot exchanges. A good ceiling shot must be returned by another good ceiling shot, even if it's growing dark and the score is only 3-2.

7. Be ready to cross over and save a shot that passes your partner. After all, you cover the whole court in singles.

8. The Z-ball is a very effective weapon in doubles because it often confuses the court coverage of the opposition. There are also many more opportunities for this shot in doubles because of side-court positioning.

9. Communicate with your partner *during* the play. In singles, talking or shouting during the course of a rally is frowned upon; it's distracting, unnecessary, and unsportsmanlike. In doubles, it is not only permissible but mandatory in carrying out your strategy. To stay alive in a hectic rally you may need to call upon your partner to abandon the usual coverage to plug up a weakness. It's also helpful to announce which ceiling shots you will return when they happen to come down the middle zone.

10. Safety first. The court does not accommodate eight legs, eight arms, and four racquets very well. Serious injury can result from careless swinging.

4

Practice

Behind any great athlete is practice. The glitter and the gold are never the result of good fortune; they are richly deserved. Although it has become somewhat fashionable for a few of the top stars to portray themselves as "casual" heroes—beer-drinking, party-going rowdies—the whole image is fraudulent. If they have achieved limelight stature, it's the result of practice, practice, practice, not of extracurricular escapades. Dedication and superb conditioning are always there, even if they choose to flash a different facade for public consumption.

A few years ago Jack Nicklaus described his practice technique prior to a victory in the U.S. Open. Among other drills, he hit five sand shots out of *every* trap on the golf course one day. That amounted to 550 sand shots! The story has a happy ending, as do most Golden Bear tales. During the four-day tournament he landed in sixteen bunkers. Fifteen times he was able to get up and down in two strokes. That drill probably won the tournament.

Former national champion Charlie Brumfield has been known to practice one shot a thousand times without a break. And then move on to another and do the same.

119

Total concentration is evident as this player sets up for a forehand drive.

The message is clear. The more you practice, the better you play. And the better you play, the more fun you have. Having a gift is one thing; developing it to the fullest, and seeing it flower, is another.

Although the best time to practice a shot is right after you miss it, you don't have that privilege in a match. When you serve 2 inches shy for a short-corner ace, you can't try it again for fear of double-faulting. And you can't concentrate on form if you have to be concerned with the outcome of the shot. In match play, form should be the farthest thing from your mind. But good form becomes natural only after you've worked at it over and over in practice.

Let's not pretend that practice is fun. We'd all rather play. The problem of monotony in practice is a challenge to anyone's ingenuity. Imaginary gaming techniques may be needed to soup up the action and keep you from being bored to death. Anything is worthwhile that will divert your attention from the dismal reality that you are repeating the same motion like an obsessive automaton. You'll need a dose of self-deception to "enjoy" practicing.

Practice methods should be designed to fit practice goals. Some things are best worked out alone on the court. Others fit better into a two-player routine. Still others cannot be developed unless live play is in progress. These three settings are all useful in their own right and will be discussed separately.

SOLO PRACTICE

I had originally planned to include a suggestion for a rigid one-hour practice drill, but I realized that I had never adhered to one myself. So you are on your own, but remember to spend your practice time productively. Work on the areas of your game that need the most help.

Before moving on to actual drills, a few general rules are in order:

1. Use your time well. You aren't paid by the hour, but by the quality of the product. Have some definite purpose in mind when you practice.

2. Keep in mind the value of both general and specific practice. Some days you may work a full-circuit routine. Other days you might devote the whole time to improving a single shot.

3. Keep it simple—as you will if you follow my recommendations in this section. (Some drills I've seen in print would qualify you for a Ph.D. in physics.)

4. Spend most of the time on your weaknesses, not on your strengths. Why is it that the best kill shooters persist in hitting mainly kill shots? It's

stupid. Admittedly, it's more enjoyable to do what you're good at, but it won't make you a better player. Work on what you *can't* do well.

5. Use live balls. There's a tendency in all sports to practice with old used equipment. That's all right for your shag bag in golf, but in this game you're taking a big risk. During solo practice you hit as many as five times the number of shots you hit in the same time span while playing; that is, you hit five hours' worth of shots in one hour. This is no time to save money: Try to get away with using dead balls so intensively and you might throw your arm out. Cortisone shots cost more than live balls.

Warmup Drill

Take a center position at three-quarter court depth. Hit a medium-hard forehand shot about 3 feet high on the front wall just to the left of center, so that it rebounds on one hop to your backhand. Then hit a similar backhand shot so that it returns to your forehand. See how long you can keep it going with control. It's tougher than you think. Concentrate on form, footwork, and body action. Be sure to take a full pivot with each shot, then a full follow-through, and return to the face-front position. This exercise will also help you adjust to the slight grip rotation needed in going from forehand to backhand and back again. You must learn to hit the strokes right before you start going for kill shots.

Passing-Shot Drill

Take a center position just behind the short line. Hit a soft shot to the front wall that rebounds to your forehand. Hit a sharp pass down the right side (down-the-wall pass) so that it hugs the wall all the way. Repeat several times.

Subdivide the cross-court pass into two types. The first should rebound parallel with the left side wall as a mirror image of the down-the-wall pass. The second should be angled more sharply so as to hit the side wall in the service area (V-pass). Repeat several times. Then practice the same three shots with the backhand stroke.

Repeat the whole exercise on shots rebounding off the *back* wall.

On all passing shots, keep in mind that the most common error is hitting

"Always practice up to the level of your own ability."

the ball too high—giving the opponent a second chance off the back wall. Be sure your target on the front wall is no more than 2–3 feet high. Then watch carefully to see that your passing shots don't hit the back wall before the second bounce.

Kill-Shot Drill

Some authors recommend the "drop-and-hit" drill, in which you simply drop the ball from your hand and hit a kill shot. I think it's a poor drill, too far removed from reality. It's far better to practice your kill shots on live setups. Simulate actual play as closely as possible. First the forehand:

1. Hit a soft shot to the right front wall that rebounds no farther than the short line. Set up and kill to the right corner. Repeat and vary the depth.

2. Hit a soft ceiling shot that rebounds into the same area. Set up and kill to the right corner. Repeat and vary the depth.

3. Hit a medium-hard shot to the front wall near the corner so that it ricochets off the side wall to your forehand at mid-court. Set up and kill to the right corner. Repeat and vary the depth.

4. Hit a hard shot high off the right front wall so as to carry to the back wall on the fly. Follow the ball as it bounds forward, wait for the bounce and drop, then set up and kill to the right corner. Repeat.

5. Hit a hard ceiling shot on the right side so that it bounces off the back wall. Follow the path of the ball, set up and kill to the right corner. (This is a much tougher shot than the last because you have to hit it before the bounce.) Repeat.

These five setup positions will cover most of your kill-shot chances in racquetball. But they are different shots, so practice them as separate entities. Mix in a few cross-court kills to the opposite corner, but don't spend too much time on these. In actual play, 90 percent or more should be hit to the near corner.

Repeat the whole exercise on the backhand side.

Your target for kill shots should be the corner, 6–12 inches above the floor. Aim for an area rather than a spot. Some try to jazz it up a bit by using an open box for a target, or stacked cans. If you're advanced enough to divide your kill shots into straight kill, pinch, and reverse pinch, do it. Always practice up to the level of your own ability.

Ceiling-Shot Drill

Ceiling-shot drill is perpetual. It's perpetual because a perfect ceiling shot to the left side almost demands the same return. It's ideal for solo practice. And so important. See how many perfect backhand ceiling shots you can hit along the left wall without catching that wall or rebounding too deep off the back wall. First pay attention to the depth, then the angle. Then both. Try to wallpaper every shot.

Now and then, hit a few cross-court, to the right side and back, with your forehand—but remember that the bulk of your ceiling-shot practice should be backhands to the left corner.

Z-Ball Drill

Hit a soft ceiling shot to the left side that comes up shallow near the short line. Hit a perfect backhand Z-ball to the left rear corner. Try to drive the ball deep —as close to the back wall as possible without hitting it. Repeat. Then do the same on the right side with the forehand. (You might also combine this drill with the previous ceiling-shot drill; each time a ceiling ball comes up short, hit the Z-ball.)

AWB Drill

Hit a ceiling shot that comes back to three-quarter court depth on the left. Hit a perfect backhand AWB to the right rear corner. Repeat. Then do the same with the forehand on the right side. (You might also combine this drill with the ceiling-shot drill for variety.) Concentrate on the height and depth of this shot. The object is to hit the second side wall high, just past the short line— deep enough not to give an immediate setup, yet not so deep as to come off the back wall for a delayed setup.

BUDDY PRACTICE

Most drills are more fun with a partner. You probably won't have one available as often as you'd like, but when you do, you can help each other work on your respective needs. Suggested drills:

Serve-and-Return Drill

The serve-and-return drill is easily the most important drill of all. As discussed earlier, the serve return is the most important shot in the game, but you need a partner, since you can't very well practice serve returns without someone to do the serving. If you practice serving alone, you spend half the time chasing the balls around.

Work on all varieties of serve. Use this time to hone down the finer points of angle and depth. You have a chance to concentrate, because for the moment you don't have to be concerned with the return. This is the time to develop the short-corner serve for that moment when you badly need an ace. Refine the subtle variations of the Z-serve so that no two are exactly alike. Also, work on improving your serve to the right side without setting yourself up for a blistering return.

Now change positions and work on your serve returns. Your principal focus should be on hitting perfect ceiling shots to the left corner with consistency. But you also take advantage of this type of practice to work on kill-shot returns and cross-court passes. Experiment against the Z-serve. Take a few in the air *before* they hit the floor or the side wall, and a few after. Try some Z-balls and AWBs for serve return variety.

If you've been blowing the returns on soft Z-serves to the right side, ask your partner to hit a few dozen. You'll be better at it the next time.

Kill-and-Retrieve Drill

A lot of players don't go after kill shots they might get to. Not because they're lazy, but because they never actually learn the potential range of their coverage. The kill-and-retrieve drill is a good way to discover that range. Another thing that will come as a surprise—even a shock—to most players is that kill shots come out much farther than it seems. Take a few minutes and watch a game sometime with this in mind. Take note of how far the ball comes out before hitting the floor a second time. You'll find that the great majority, except for rollouts, will reach the service line—and I'm referring to *good* kill shots, not poor ones. Most of us are so frozen in place by the sight of a kill shot hitting low on the front wall that we don't react quickly enough to even cover the service-line area. Keep this in mind and it will take a lot of the pressure off. It isn't necessary to reach the front wall to retrieve kill shots. Just cover the service-line area and you'll get to most of them.

Hit soft ceiling shots that come up shallow near the short line. Your partner should respond with kill shots, and you try to retrieve *every one*—even those you don't think you can reach. Try a kill if you have a full stroke. If not, practice the drop shot. This is a good drill to develop mobility and anticipation —to get your body in motion *before* your partner actually hits the ball.

Switch positions and practice your kill shots while he does the digging.

Fly-Kill Drill

Hit an easy serve to the left corner. Your partner then hits a cross-court drive to your forehand. You pluck it out of the air *before* the bounce and kill to the right corner. Then serve to the right corner and practice the same shot with your backhand. Repeat.

Then change positions and practice your cross-court drives while he kills fly shots.

Reverse Back-Wall Drill

Take a position at center court near the short line. Hit a soft setup to the other player near the left side wall. He then hits a cross-court V-pass, and you whirl and try to save it with a reverse back-wall smash. Then do the same on the other side with your forehand. This is another drill in which your range of coverage will surprise you. You won't get to all the shots or even to the majority, but they will still amount to more than you would have guessed. This will help you develop a never-quit attitude toward passing shots in the future and is the major purpose of this drill, rather than the value of the shot itself.

Then change positions and give your partner the same runaround, as you practice your cross-court passes.

Cross-Court Ceiling-Shot Drill

The best way to practice the cross-court ceiling shot without wearing yourself out running back and forth is to station your partner in one rear corner, yourself in the other. Then simply hit cross-court ceiling shots over and over. This drill will prepare you for a left-handed opponent when the situation arises. He usually has a built-in advantage because his opponent isn't used to hitting cross-court backhand ceiling shots to the right corner. His backhand is rarely tested with accurate right-side ceiling shots.

Overhead Drill

One player in the service area and the other in back court. The front player hits a ceiling shot anywhere but along the left wall, allowing the rear player enough room to hit a variety of overhead kills and passes to either side. The forecourt player tries to retrieve and hit another ceiling shot. Keep on going as long as possible, aiming most of your overheads to the right corner.

Change positions and go at it again.

PRACTICE GAMES

How's your ego these days? Is it secure enough to survive an undeserved insult? Would you be crushed if a hacker ran off the court broadcasting his hollow victory over you to the whole club? Can you swallow a little pride and be satisfied with the knowledge that you could have beaten him if you had to?

Call it character building, if you will, but that's what it takes to get the most out of practice games on the way to future rewards. You must be willing to lose to a lesser player once in a while as you engage in "live" practice. If you rely exclusively on your strong points during practice games, you'll never get any better. You must work on new shots and weaknesses every time you play. You can't join the backhand kill-shot club until you hit your "initiation fee" into the floor a few thousand times. You can't develop an aggressive serving game without variety, and you achieve this only by working some new serves into your practice games. Sure, you'll set up a few choice pumpkins in the process. But that's how you learn. It's all worth it. You have to pay your dues to add a new dimension to your game. And when you beat the club kingpin someday, the echoes of that worthless hacker will quickly fade.

Always play with a plan. It's a terrible waste to spend an hour of time and effort on the court without planting at least a smidgen of long-term investment. Have a few objectives in mind—but not too many. There is such a thing as "overthink":

> The centipede was happy, quite
>   Until a toad in fun
> Said, "Pray, which leg goes after which?"
> This worked his mind to such a pitch
> He lay distracted in a ditch,
>   Considering how to run.

Take a lesson from the poor centipede: Don't clutter your mind with too many things—just two or three each time you play. One time you might try to hit perfect left-side ceiling shots against all serves, while going cross-court on most kill shots. Next time out you might return all serves with cross-court drives and down-the-wall kills, while hitting V-passes on offensive chances.

Always select one serve to perfect, even though you serve a variety. And don't be afraid to serve up a few right-side serves to the local forehand kill-shot artist. You'll pay the penalty for a bad serve in a hurry. It is the quick way to learn not to hit bad serves.

Now let's presume you've done your homework, come up with a good experimental pregame plan, and then played the game. Finished? Not yet. The most important pledge is still to be taken: the postmortem analysis and critique. Don't subject yourself to the pain and sacrifice of making from five hundred to a thousand shots, only to flush out your brain in the shower. Sit down later and play the game over in your head, give yourself the old armchair instant replay so as to arrive at some plan for next time. Think about the quality of every aspect of your game. Most players never have the faintest idea why they lose. And they keep on losing. Heed thou the word of the sage Santayana: "Those who cannot remember the past are condemned to repeat it." If the old philosopher wasn't talking about racquetball, he might just as well have been.

Checklist of Key Points

You might even want to use a checklist of some sort. Here's one I use:

SERVES
1. Was every serve in your arsenal used at least once?
2. Which serves led to setups?
3. Which serves led to kill-shot returns?
4. Were you keeping the serves off the back wall?
5. Were your second serves of good quality?
6. Did you get caught fading or drifting?
7. Which serve will you work on next time?

SERVE RETURNS
1. Did you get aced by playing back too far?
2. Were you left with no shots in the corner on lob serves because you failed to move up to hit them on the fly?
3. Were your cross-court drives wide enough? And low enough?
4. Did you move up quickly after every offensive return?

5. Did you punish (or even notice) drifting and fading?
6. Which serves caused you the most trouble in moving the server into the back court?
7. Which serves were the most difficult to return with good ceiling shots?

OFFENSE
1. Were your kill shots coming in too high or too low?
2. Did you hit a few cross-court kills from both sides?
3. Did you shoot the backhand kill every time the shot was called for? Or did you cop out with the cross-court pass?
4. How many fly kills did you jump on?
5. Any overhead kills or passes?
6. Were your passing shots wide enough?
7. Did you keep your passing shots off the back wall?
8. Did you follow your cross-court passes with a lateral move?
9. Did you try any drop shots?
10. Did you move with the ball on back-wall shots?

DEFENSE
1. Were your ceiling shots consistently in the left corner with good depth? Did you force backhand returns? How many wallpapers did you hit?
2. Did you get back into good position after *every* ceiling shot, or were you caught napping by overhead winners?
3. Were your Z-balls deep enough?
4. Were your AWBs too deep?
5. Did you get boxed in by your own Z-balls or AWBs?
6. Did you save any "lost" passing shots with reverse back-wall smashes? Did you even try?
7. Did you make an early charge on the other player's kill-shot setups?

Discipline yourself. Answer questions like these before you deem yourself ready to play again. It's a good idea to go over the same list after tournament games.

In summary, stay with your strength at tournament time, but bend over backward to avoid your best shots during practice games. Hit your weaknesses. Don't worry about losing that practice match. It doesn't bother Marty Hogan. And you can't find much more ego than that, pardner.

Speed and endurance may not always be enough. Sometimes you even have to fly. Note the perfect horizontal the diving player makes in saving the point.

5

Conditioning for Racquetball

Fatigue is the assassin of the racquetball player, a foe more dangerous than your opponent. No matter how perfect your strategy, no matter how probing your insights, it's all useless if you're too tired to execute. Theory won't save you from the penalties of being unfit. You can't hit a kill shot if you don't have the energy to pivot, set your feet, and lean into the stroke. You can't hit a ceiling shot if you don't have the strength to raise your arm. You can't run if you can't breathe.

If you're in poor shape, you'll lose an even match—and, what's worse, you're apt to get hurt. Injuries don't just happen; they occur as a direct result of exhaustion. You're much more likely to develop a malignant case of the trips and the fumbles when you're pooped out. Statistics show clearly the increase in both the number and severity of injuries in the *later* stages of football and basketball games. As the players get more tired, they make more errors; when they make errors, they get hurt.

Conditioning is not an absolute prerequisite for racquetball. For those who wish to stroll onto the court, pat the ball around for a while, and call it a day—so be it. On the other hand, why not take a walk in the park instead? But if you enjoy competition, you have to get into shape for this game.

131

"The day you become a bonafide racquetball player is the day you decide to get into shape to play racquetball rather than playing racquetball to get into shape."

REWARDS OF CONDITIONING

The day you become a bona fide racquetball player is the day you decide to get into shape to play racquetball rather than playing racquetball to get into shape. Make no mistake about this: The primary purpose of conditioning is not just to retrieve more shots but to improve the quality of your play. It takes energy and movement to turn your body, set your feet, and make a shot correctly, and the first flaw to appear in a tired player is hitting the ball without setting up. But with better shotmaking as the goal of conditioning the ability to retrieve more shots will follow naturally.

The benefits of conditioning go far beyond the game alone. Just to name a few:

Heart Strength
The finely tuned athlete has fewer heart attacks. Even more striking is the survival rate; he's more likely to get out alive if he has one. In every field of comparison, exercise is the key determinant. Whatever your occupation, you'll be healthier if you exercise.

Weight Control
The lazy and obese claim that exercise is useless in weight control. They rationalize that you eat more afterward, therefore accomplish nothing. Not only is that untrue, but recent evidence draws the opposite conclusion. Vigorous activity has the immediate effect of inhibiting both appetite and food intake. The mechanism is twofold: first, fluid replacement is in itself quite filling; second, exercise raises the blood-sugar level, thereby reducing the craving for food. Furthermore, motivation for weight control increases right along with conditioning. After all, it's harder work to play racquetball or run if you're overweight.

Muscle Tone

Firming up of muscles occurs as flabbiness fades, even if there is no weight change.

Tension Control

One of the most neglected areas of study in medical research is the effect of emotional stress on physical ailments. We have good evidence that stress contributes heavily to high blood pressure, heart disease, peptic ulcers, colitis, migraine headaches, and mental illness; but how many others might there be? Physical fitness eases tension, increases the ability to cope with stress, and makes each of the above less likely to happen.

Psychological Uplift

The joy of achievement affects all other aspects of life. Your overall attitude changes every time you set up a new challenge and meet it. Fitness is no exception. When you succeed in one thing, you're more likely to succeed in the next.

Other Sports

Being in good shape must add a plus to any other game you play. I'm certain that the leg power from racquetball and running has added extra yards to my tee shots. And the myth that playing one racquet sport harms your play in another has been laid to rest. If anything, racquetball will make you a *better* tennis player.

Evolution is no longer working in our favor. A few million years ago, we were almost guaranteed genetic sanction. Our fathers survived because they were in good enough shape to escape predators—and fast enough to catch our mothers. Today the most vigorous pursuit of the average citizen is the walk from the car to the elevator. Even in heavy industry most of the real work is done by machines. Most distressing of all is to see physical laziness spreading to our youth. They get less exercise than their parents. How many sixteen-year-olds do you know whose bikes have been gathering dust since the day they got their driver's licenses?

It may take a bit of a push to get started—to overcome the epidemic inertia of a sedentary society. But it must be done. Get moving.

TRAINING

Is Homo sapiens a quitter? I think not. Then why do so many fitness programs start with a bang and end with a whimper? Why are 95 percent of the "I'm going to whip myself into shape" New Year's resolutions forgotten before the Ides of March? I don't think people are inherently lazy by nature. When they begin a program with enthusiasm and high goals—and then quit—there have to be reasons. They go like this:

> They quit because they don't get results.
> They don't get results because they train *poorly*.
> They train poorly because they don't understand the principles.
> And neither do most of the fitness manuals.

Nobody in his right mind is going to persist in a program that brings no success. That's why there are so many dropouts. The intentions are good, the methods are bad. The work is tedious, the gratification nil.

If this country ever does attain a respectable level of fitness, there should be a national holiday of thanks to Dr. Kenneth Cooper of the Aerobics Center in Dallas. His masterpiece, *Aerobics* (1968), ranks on the list of investigative breakthroughs right next to Darwin and Kinsey. The information he published at the end of a long and careful study of action physiology made it possible for all of us to understand what really happens, to act accordingly—that is, correctly—and, most of all, to get results.

Olympic records are now being smashed regularly in every event. Remember the excitement over the first sub-4-minute mile? Now it's not uncommon for a man to run a 3:59 mile and finish dead last. Man's body has not been suddenly born better after a million years. Our nutrition is not the answer. The clocks aren't getting slower. There's only one difference:

We're learning how to train.

Your body is not the body of a lifeless statue. You're not stiff, wooden, and unyielding. You're a mass of muscles and joints that were made to move. Effortlessly. Easily. Gracefully. Nothing is more beautiful than slow-motion films of the human body in athletic pursuit. Unfortunately, our sedentary way of life stifles the natural impulse to get up and go. It is a sad commentary that it takes such concentrated effort to neutralize this influence—to have to urge the body on to do what it was born to do.

Fitness means different things to different people. To the high-school teenager it means being fit enough to make the varsity. To the middle-aged it means being fit enough to halt the weight shift to the waistline. Later it means being fit enough to keep up with the demands of job and leisure time without having a coronary. For us racquetball players, fitness will mean one thing only —endurance—the ability to last.

Cast off, just for now, any preconceived ideas of what fitness has meant to you. Explore a system that may revolutionize your whole approach to the subject. Fitness will be the end result of a scientific method of endurance training. Even if you were never to pick up a racquet, you'd gain something valuable through the enlightenment of the modern concept of fitness.

ENDURANCE TRAINING

Activity requires energy. The body produces energy by burning food. The fuel is oxygen. The body can store the food, but it can't store the oxygen. It must replenish its supply constantly. The challenge begins here.

Most of us can punch out enough energy to perform our ordinary chores. But as the activity becomes more vigorous, some can't keep up. The delivery of oxygen falls behind the demands for energy. The spread between minimum requirements and maximum ability on demand is the real meaning of physical fitness. The fit have the greatest spread, the ability to reach out for more. The unfit have no reserve to draw upon.

Consider the nature of a physical act, whether it's hitting a shot, taking a step, or pulling up your socks. This is the final step in a chain of events that might be simplified as follows:

Air → lungs → bloodstream → muscle → POW!

You breathe in the air. The oxygen is absorbed through the pulmonary alveoli (lung minisacs) into the circulating blood. Then the heart takes over. Its job is to pump the blood around and deliver the oxygen to the muscle, where it can be used for energy. The key is in the delivery of the oxygen from the air you've breathed in to the tissues. What we call fatigue is brought on by the failure of the delivery system to keep up with the demands for energy. Don't be sucked in by the glamor of body-building, isometrics, and calisthenics. The way to endurance is through the buildup of the heart-lung system. You can spend half your waking hours pumping up arm and leg muscles, but it all goes for naught if you can't get the oxygen to those muscles when you need it. The heart-lung system should be the focal point of every conditioning system.

Progress is measured best by the ability to consume oxygen. The practical way to monitor this is to be aware of heart action. To evaluate the worth of your training, count the heart rate—pulse rate—*while* you are training. These next few paragraphs may read like a ledger in medical accounting, but it's time to put the generalities aside and get down to specifics. To do this we must talk numbers.

At rest the pulse rate of the average person is 70–75 beats per minute. Add physical action and the rate starts rising. The need for oxygen goes up. The heart-lung machine tries to supply it. The ability to maintain a high pulse rate for long periods of time is the definition of fitness. But the numbers are critical, so take note of these three specific conclusions of reliable research:

1. Whatever the exercise, to qualify as training the pulse rate must rise to at least 150 beats per minute, and preferably to 180. If you don't get it up that high, you're wasting your time. (Healthy hearts will peak out at about 190 beats per minute. Damaged hearts, when stressed, will go as high as 220, which is dangerous to say the least. The unfit cannot sustain the rate. The fit can and do. However, allowances are made for age. If you're above forty, set your goal at 75 percent of 220 minus age.)

2. The increase must be maintained at the above rate for at least 15–30 minutes. If it's less than that, you're wasting your time. Real training doesn't even begin to take place until *after* 5 minutes of a high rate.

3. It must challenge the system *beyond* the threshold of tolerance. The only way to strengthen a system is to overload it. If you're not short of breath, with your heart pounding, your blood surging through your veins, you're wasting your time.

Obviously, you're not going to be able to trot out to the gym and achieve this on the spot if you haven't been training already. That's a good way to kill yourself. You have to work up to it gradually and sensibly. But the goals are clear-cut. Whether you play or run or ride a stationary bike—try to get your heart rate up to 180 and keep it there for 15–30 minutes. You simply can't measure the value of your training program until you start counting heartbeats. Get back on the right track to fitness. Do anything that will demand oxygen, then force your body to process and deliver it. Marathon runners are able to maintain heart rates of 170 for 2–3 hours at a time on cross-country runs.

Here's what happens as you train:

1. You increase your lung power—process more air with less effort—twice as much as the unfit.

2. You increase your heart power—pump more blood per stroke (stroke volume).

3. You decrease your resting heart rate. Count your pulse. Mine is 45. So is John Havlicek's. We play different games, but the training principles are the same. The stronger your heart gets, the less often it has to pump to get the job done. The difference with training can add up to a saving of 25,000 beats per day!

4. You increase your collateral circulation—the number and size of the blood vessels carrying the blood to the tissues (including the circulation to the heart muscle itself).

5. You increase your total blood volume—by as much as one full quart.

6. You improve your muscle tone—from flabby to firm.

7. You convert fat weight to lean weight.

The ultimate goal of endurance training is to be able to perform the task, in this case racquetball, without huffing and puffing. But it takes a lot of huffs and puffs to get there.

Some players stay fit with racquetball alone. This can be done—but only if each game is approached with the discipline of a workout. The training principle must never leave the player's mind: to raise the heart rate to 180 and keep it there. That means you'll have a real problem on your hands if your opponent is a weaker player. You're going to get a few strange looks as you keep on charging around the court after the point is over—or digging after shots that he's already missed, and so forth. If you don't do those things, you won't be able to sustain the necessary heart rate. You'll be playing but not training. (Some guys "play" seven days a week and never do get into shape—and just can't understand it.) Besides, this kind of workout gets to be an awful chore; it takes the pure fun out of the game.

There are also some perfectly respectable exercises that can be mentioned as not providing a real workout for racquetball.

What Isn't Endurance Training

The following activities all have some value in the total scheme of physical fitness. But racquetball is a sport that demands endurance, and none of these activities ranks very high in developing the endurance necessary for an action sport. My comments are not intended as a put-down, but rather a clarification of the realistic objectives of each area of exercise.

Calisthenics

Go ahead and do those 50 situps every day for good muscle tone and potbelly prevention—but don't kid yourself—calisthenics is not training for endurance sports. General exercises do little to develop cardiorespiratory efficiency.

Isometrics

The most abused and least understood of all exercises, isometrics may lead to a substantial increase in the *bulk* of muscles, but without a parallel gain in cardiac power. Muscular strength per se has little influence on the endurance of the heart-lung system. Heart rate may go up but is not maintained. Isometrics are useful primarily in strengthening a specific muscle group or rehabilitating a damaged part—after an injury, a stroke, polio, et cetera.

Body Building

Sorry, but the perfect-looking body is no indication of endurance fitness. It's a by-product. Being too musclebound can actually reduce agility. The real key is elsewhere. As a fitness method it's worse than nothing because it makes you think you're more fit than you really are.

Running is the best conditioner for racquetball. Here, the author chugs along in his never-ending effort to gain that one-step advantage on his four-wall foes.

Golf, bowling, casual biking, and so forth rarely give a heart rate above 100. Even baseball and football, though productive of high rates briefly, never sustain the rate more than a few seconds. Fun, but little endurance fitness.

Casual Racquetball

If you play with someone inferior—and loaf—you won't raise your heart rate enough to qualify as a legitimate workout. To the man who says, "I play five times a week; how come I'm in such poor shape?" the reply should be, "With whom?"

Slooow Jogging

Unless you monitor your heart rate to have objective proof of endurance training, the benefits of jogging may be an illusion. Jogging is not necessarily running. Your pulse may never go up past 120, making it a useless exercise. However, it may be properly alternated with running, as described below.

RUNNING

Running is an essential part of the training program for those inflicted with four-wall madness. There are simply no tricks or gimmicks to replace running. You can let court savvy and positional cleverness support you up to a point; likewise, you can psych yourself up—but only so far; sooner or later the demon of conditioning will prod you with a vengeance. You must run.

Runners now number 8 million, plus countless others who move along at a faster pace over longer distances. Jogging routes have been set up in cities all across the United States. There were 150 marathons run last year—an increase of 500 percent in only five years. Muggers have become terrified of being trampled to death by little old ladies in sweat suits running in the park.

The ongoing debate over the relative value of sprints versus long-distance running will never be resolved. Both sides are correct. Both methods are necessary. Long-distance running is needed to prepare for the inevitable marathon match. Sprints are needed because they come closer to the actual challenge of racquetball. A mixture of the two is better yet—alternating slow jogs and quick sprints for about 50 yards each, for several miles if you can hack it. Or else try some "buildups"—slow jog → fast trot → sprint → fast trot → slow jog, and so forth.

Don't lose sight of our fundamental thesis of fitness training. Whatever running program you adopt, you must determine the effect it has on your pulse rate in order to place a value on it. If you tippy-toe around the neighborhood in your tiger-striped Adidas with a heart rate of 120, you might just as well sit on the porch and watch the trucks go by. You're training for chess, not racquetball. Remember the three basic rules as you run: Push to a pulse of 150–180; maintain it for at least 15–30 minutes; strain hard enough to cause some distress. Unless you force yourself *beyond* the point of previous highs, you won't make progress. If you don't run against the clock, don't bother to run.

Let me offer two suggestions on accurate pulse counting. First of all, the best artery to use is the carotid. This can be easily found in the neck just below the angle of the jaw. Second, it's important to count for only *six seconds* and multiply by ten to arrive at a rate per minute. When you engage in strenuous activity and then ease up, the rate begins to taper off rapidly. If you were to count the pulse for a full minute after you ease up, you would get an inaccurate reading—far below the actual pulse rate during peak activity.

If you have any desire to play tournaments, you'll have to go one step further. You might be called upon to play several times in one day. You guessed it. You have to play or run several times a day to get ready. Run before you play. Run after you play. The pros do it.

ARM AND LEG POWER

Arm Exercises

A long match against a defensive player with a good ceiling game can wear out your shooting arm. You might lose even if you're the better player, since he merely outlasts you. Immunize yourself against this pestilence with a simple program of arm-strengthening exercises.

There are three basic arm motions used in shooting racquetball: forehand, backhand, and overhead. Use a system that simulates these motions as closely as possible. The "universal gym" type of apparatus with the hand pulley is ideal for this purpose. With the grip handle attached to the floor-level pulley, three exercises get right to the point:

Forehand pulley exercise

Forehand Pulley Exercise

Stand sideways with your shooting arm next to the equipment. Grasp the handle loosely at your hip. Now pull upward across your chest to the other shoulder and back again (simulating a forehand stroke against resistance). Repeat several times.

Backhand Pulley Exercise

Do the same exercise as the forehand, facing the opposite way. Start by reaching across your body to grasp the handle at the opposite hip. Then pull across and upward until your arm is fully extended straight out from your body at shoulder height (simulating a backhand stroke against resistance). Repeat several times. If you need convincing as to the importance of weight shift in shotmaking, try this exercise with your forward foot off the floor. All power is lost.

Overhead Pulley Exercise

Lie flat, legs extended straight out away from the equipment. Reach back over your head and grasp the handle with your arm fully extended. Now pull upward and forward until your hand is back down at your side, and then back (simulating an overhead against resistance). Repeat several times.

As you train, increase the weight resistance and the number of repeti-

Overhead pulley exercise

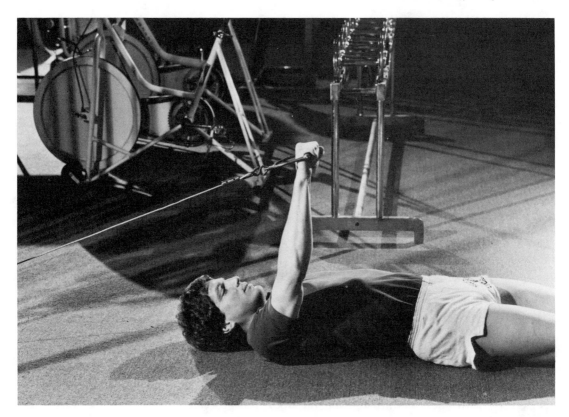

tions. Don't push too hard at first, or you'll end up with pulled muscles and tendonitis. Start with no more than 10–20 pounds and ten repetitions. Step it up systematically according to tolerance.

You're not done yet. The above will power up your arm and shoulder, but won't do much for wrist action. Supplement with a series of wrist curls, using a lightweight barbell, and you'll round out the program.

Wrist curls

Wrist curls

Leg Exercises

Gordie Howe always said the whip in his slap shot came from his legs, not his arms. Watch Nolan Ryan, one of the fastest pitchers in baseball, "push off" the pitching mound. If you still have any doubt about the need for strong legs, take a look at the tree-trunk thighs of the racquetball pros the next time they stump through town.

Developing leg power gives you double benefits. Your endurance will be improved and so will your shooting. Three basic exercises are recommended:

Leg Press

Sit with your back firmly against the seat and your hands holding the seat rails. Press your feet against the pedals until your legs are fully extended. Return to the starting position, maintaining the tension on the weights. Repeat several times. Start with whatever weight is comfortable, and work up.

Leg press

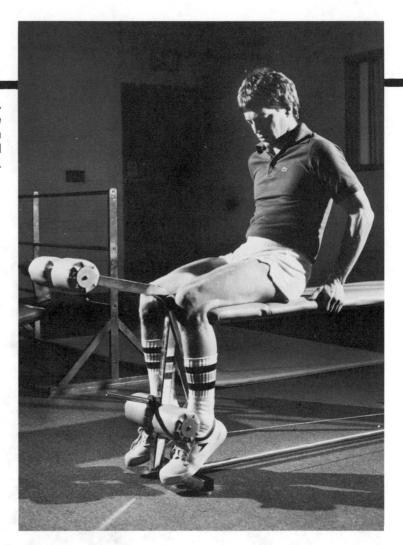

Knee extensions. Note the muscle definition developed around the knee joint.

Leg Extensions

Lock both feet under the lower rollers at the thigh-knee station. Pull up until your legs are fully extended, parallel with the floor. Return to the starting position with firm control of the weights. Start with 20 pounds and work up. This is a great one for prevention of knee injuries.

Stationary Bike Riding

If you can't do stationary bike riding against a hefty resistance, skip it. Set the resistance high enough so that it takes everything you've got to push those pedals.

TRAINING SCHEDULES

Choose the time for your workouts with a few facts in mind. Experts on physical performance have found that the peak of human efficiency is reached 3–4 hours after the previous meal. This would point to the customary noontime and five-o'clock workouts as making pretty good sense. Note, however, that the early-morning hours would not fit in with these conclusions. Moderate wake-up exercises are OK, but don't overdo it. I, for one, have always viewed strenuous exercise at dawn as somewhere between barbaric and insane. There are those who swear by it, but the bulk of the evidence indicates that it's unphysiologic and unwise.

Having been a noontime napper for years, I've always preferred 5:00 P.M. as the best time to play or work out. Don't let the tired feeling at the end of a day's work hold you back. It's probably more mental than physical. If anything, it ought to give you more reason to let off steam. Most surprising of all, you will feel less tired *after* exercising than you felt before—in spite of having expended energy in the process. Take that, Isaac Newton!

As to frequency, one rule must be emphasized: If you can't exercise regularly, you're better off not to exercise at all. Sad but true. It's dangerous to subject your heart to "occasional" stress without preparation. The older you get, the more the rule applies. As you get up in years, play more often or don't play at all. Cut out, but don't cut down.

If the goal is to improve endurance fitness, training should take place at least five times a week. If the goal is merely to stay even, three times a week will do. Anything less will cause you to slip. None of the pros advise playing the game every day. They usually stick with an equal split of three days playing–three days running, or something of the sort.

Whatever your schedule, keep yourself in shape all year around. Don't let your reserves dwindle. It's far easier to *maintain* a level of fitness than it is to strive repeatedly to recapture what you've lost. You'd waste valuable time and energy that might be better spent on practice. Increase the work load and you gain. Sit around and do nothing, and it deteriorates. It's as simple as that. You can't collect and store fitness like master points. It must be fed and nurtured regularly.

There's no point in playing the fitness game if you don't keep score. If you're serious, keep some records. A large calendar or small diary will do. For one thing, the illusion of "regular" workouts can deceive even the most honest. Write down the dates and achievements. You might find to your embarrassment that you haven't been as dedicated as you thought.

Another benefit in keeping records is that you have a chance to watch your progress—graphically. And to be smug. You can't help but gloat a bit as you glance back over a few months of a fitness program and see those logged-in running miles go from half a mile to 2 miles and now 5 miles. And to see your per-mile pace drop from 12 minutes to 8 to 6½. You'll find that your potential was far greater than you dreamed; if you hadn't written it down, you never would have believed it. The evidence of your own progress provides you with further get-up-and-go fuel and lends added impetus to your charge. You need to see that your labors bear fruit.

Warning: Don't let the "plateau phenomenon" get you down. Weight watchers know that pounds don't fall off in a straight line. They might lose a pound a week for three weeks, then nothing the fourth and fifth, even though there's no letdown in their efforts. Stabilizing influences constantly interfere. The result is progress, progress, no progress; progress, progress, no progress. The same principle applies in training. At certain points it will seem as if you've reached a barrier that you can't get through—you'll see no improvement for days or weeks. Well, hang in there! There is no limit to how far you can go. The gains will begin to show up again if you persist.

FOOD, VITAMINS, AND WATER

On the subject of diet, I must take a stand. At the risk of drawing the wrath of the AMA and offending those incurable health-food nuts and vitamin freaks, I'll say this to the rest of you: IGNORE THE MADNESS!

With an energy matched only by the quest for the Holy Grail, athletes and their trainers have searched for years for a "super diet." Everything from queen-bee extract to ground apricot pits has been tried. Unfortunately, the power of faith is such that the illusion of improvement sometimes occurs. But there is no proof that physiological performance is enhanced in any way.

As for the vitamin racket, and a racket it is, 99 percent of the $2 billion spent annually by the American public goes for naught. It's superfluous, going on through you like a road runner, without a pause. As soon as your kids are old enough to gum down their solid foods, they don't need vitamins. If you can eat, you don't need vitamins. Period.

Oh, it's all harmless enough, that's true. I object because it diverts the attention of the athlete away from areas that are more important. The cult would have you believe that diet and pills can fill in the gaps left by poor training. It's a cop-out for hard work.

Finally, a word on water. One of the cruel jokes played on the athlete through the years has been the advice of the "experts" not to drink water while exercising. You've all seen badly dehydrated sportsmen take a swig of H_2O, then spit it out before a drop could filter down the gullet, as if it contained deadly cyanide. Ridiculous. A few years ago, a research team checked it out and found the idea to be worse than nonsense—it is downright dangerous. Drink all the water you need to replace your losses. And you can swallow it, too.

INJURIES

Although in theory racquetball is a non-contact sport, it can be a bit unkind to your body. In terms of physical demands, it amounts to a Herculean challenge. It's a game of sudden starts and stops, twists and turns, dives and crashes. The most common injury in four-wall sports is the sprain—usually the ankle or knee. This also happens to be the injury that most often receives the wrong first-aid treatment. How many times have you seen an athlete sprain his ankle and be immediately attended to with an ice pack? Dead wrong! The ice pack is all right for later, but the very first move—which is the most important— should be *pressure*. As soon as a sprain occurs, blood flows into the tissues from ruptured blood vessels, along with edema (watery fluid) from damaged tissues. The swelling can be held down as much as 90 percent if firm pressure is applied right away. You don't need gimmicks to get the job done. Use your hands. Just grab the ankle in a stranglehold grip and hold it like a vice for ten minutes. Then wrap it firmly with an elastic bandage (Ace), but not so tight as to block the circulation. Pressure will do more to prevent the swelling than a whole bucket of ice, which you can save for the glass of Scotch you'll need later.

During the next few days, you should keep it wrapped while you're hobbling about, both for comfort and to prevent the swelling from recurring.

You may remove the wrap at bedtime, but keep it at the bedside—it's crucial that you reapply it *before* you get out of bed in the morning. If you wait until you've been on your feet for even a few minutes, you lose the benefits. It's too late to stop the swelling.

An even more common and far more picturesque insult to the racquet-ball player is the "welt-zinger," the result of being hit by the ball. This is the mark of the good positional player—the badge of honor. Beginning as a raised red ring with white center (often inspiring animal-like guttural sounds from throat and spleen), it will evolve into the blue-green-yellow spectrum in radiating patterns that would be the envy of a Renoir. Cherish those beauties. They won't be there more than two or three weeks.

Aspirin

Because it's so commonplace, aspirin has suffered a bum rap. Bearing the brunt of "Take-two-aspirins-and-call-me-in-the-morning" doctor jokes, it is, without a doubt, the most underrated medicine there is. The truth is that as a simple remedy for pain, aspirin is magic.

However, it is seldom used correctly. If you want aspirin to work, you must begin a few hours *before* the onset of the hurts, and continue with 2–3 tablets every four hours *around the clock* (there is now an eight-hour aspirin that can be used at bedtime). Three cautions should be noted:

1. *Never* take aspirin on an empty stomach. It is a highly acid substance (even the buffered form) and can eat holes in the lining of the stomach. Always down it with food and milk.
2. Don't take aspirin if you have a history of stomach or duodenal ulcers.
3. Be on the lookout for a sensation of ringing in the ears. That's the first clue that you might be taking too much for your system. This rarely occurs at the above dosage, but if it does, cut down.

Finally, a brief philosophical note. Let's not moan and groan too much about pain that is brought on by having fun, in sound mind and healthy body. Let's not lose sight of the fact that millions of people spend all their days in pain for reasons not even remotely related to pleasure. If we stop to remind ourselves of the difference, the aches will be easier to endure.

THE WARMUP

Never step onto a court without a proper warmup. You might get away with it in tennis or golf, but this game is much too physical to allow it. By getting ready to play, not only will you suffer less the next day, but you'll play better. And the older you are, the more important the warmup is. A warmup should also precede any workout, no matter how brief.

Whatever your preferences in warmup techniques, certain general principles should be followed:

1. Start slowly.
2. Gradually increase both the speed and the intensity of the exercises.
3. Try to include as many different muscle groups and joints as possible during the full course of your routine.
4. Combine muscle stretching with increased activity of the heart and lungs.

a

Arm circles. (a) Vertical; (b) horizontal

If you don't have your own set combination of warmup exercises, try the following ten-minute routine:

1. Slow jog—one minute.
2. Arm circles—one minute. Rotate the outstretched arms alternately through a full 360-degree rotation of the shoulder joint, first in a vertical plane, using backstroke and crawl swimming motions, then in a horizontal plane with arms straight out at the shoulders, making small circles clockwise and counter-clockwise. This is best done while you are walking.

b

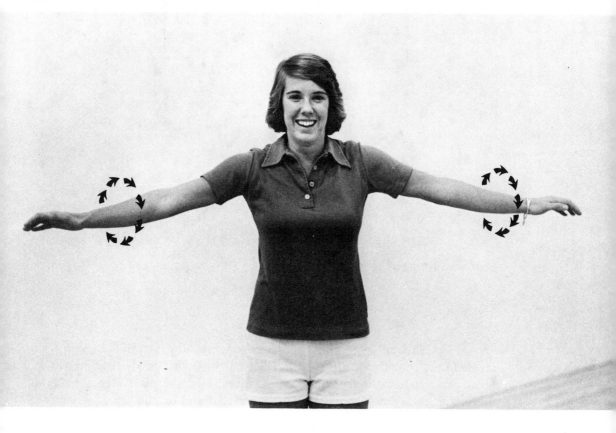

Calf and hamstring stretches

3. Calf and hamstring stretches—one minute. Stand with one foot crossed over the other, with both feet flat on the floor. Slowly reach down to touch your toes without bending your knees. Feel the pull? Repeat several times, and then cross over with your other foot and do the same.

Alternate toe touch

4. Alternate toe touch—one minute. Start with a comfortable stance, feet about 2 feet apart, and alternately touch each toe with the opposite hand. Widen your stance as you go along.

"A warmup should precede any workout, no matter how brief."

5. Half knee-bends—one minute. Start upright, feet a few inches apart, hands out in front. Keeping your back straight, slowly bend your knees to the half-squat position. Hold for a few seconds and repeat several times.

Half knee-bends

Jumping jacks

6. Jumping jacks—one minute. Stand upright, feet together and hands at your sides. Simultaneously jump your legs apart and bring your hands together above your head. Then jump back to the start position. Repeat several times.

7. Knee-chest back stretches—one minute. Lie flat. Hug *both* knees to your chest and hold for 3 seconds. Repeat several times. (Orthopedic surgeons warn against doing this exercise one knee at a time.)

**Knee-chest back
stretches**

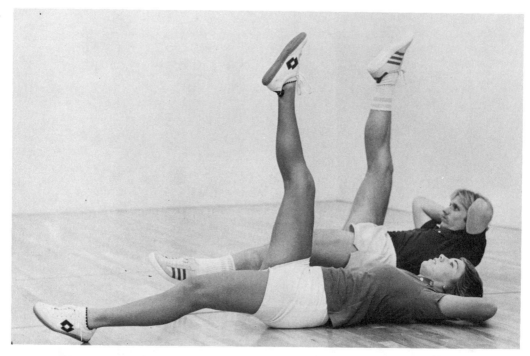

Single leg raises

8. Single leg raises—one minute. Lie flat with hands under your head. Raise one outstretched leg up to the vertical position and then back to the floor. Repeat several times. Then do the same with the other leg.

9. Hurdler's stretch—one minute. Sit on the floor, one leg outstretched, the other tucked behind you. Then touch the forward toe with the same hand, first with the fingertip and gradually as far up the hand as the wrist, if you can do it. Repeat several times and then reverse the legs. When you've finished this one, you're ready to play.

10. Fast jog—one minute.

Play ball!

Hurdler's stretch

COOLING DOWN

After a hard workout, muscles have a way of giving silent protest by tightening up—even to the point of painful spasms. To prevent this, or at least reduce it, take some time to wind down. Taper off gradually with five to ten minutes of a brisk walk or slow jog. Don't play hard for an hour and then plunk yourself down on the floor to pray for restoration. Don't run right from the court to your car. Be kind to your system by allowing a sensible, physiologic return to normalcy.

Not all muscle soreness is caused by overexertion. It might be related instead to poor warmup—or none at all. So if your time is tight, better to chop a few minutes off your playing time than to sacrifice a good warmup and wind-down.

At times the "I feel great!" result of a good workout is strangely transformed into "I feel terrible!" the next day. The worst soreness sets in about twenty-four hours after the action. The secret here is to force yourself into activity the next day. After the rigors of a tough tournament or long training session, it may be the last thing in the world you feel like doing. But do it. Go against the pleading of your natural instincts for a day off. Do some stretching exercises, a little jogging—or, even better, a lot of walking. In a recent tournament I was forced to play four matches in one day. Ordinarily, I would have been whining in pain the next day, but coincidence saved me. I had committed myself weeks before to spend that day at the Western Open golf tournament. Walking around that golf course for seven hours didn't sound too appetizing, but it worked—I had no soreness.

PEAKING FOR TOURNAMENTS

The frustration of bombing out in a tournament after playing hot the week before is one of the worst. There is no surefire way to be at your best when it means the most, but a few general hints might help with regard to the countdown days:

1. Concentrate more on training and less on playing. The tension of tournament play takes more out of you than a casual match does. You'll need to build up all the wind and legs you can muster.
2. Play with good players only. Easy matches lead to sloppy play. You

get away with too much. Get on the court with someone who will punish you for your mistakes.

3. Don't let a slump get you down. Athletes in every sport learn to cope with the peaks and valleys of performance. You might play some of your best racquetball coming off of a slump. Don't let a few bad practice matches affect your winning attitude at tournament time.

4. Stay with your strength. This is no time to experiment. As D-day approaches, try to win with what you do best.

5. No time-outs in practice matches. Challenge your endurance to the limit. This will get you ready.

6. Take a holiday the day before the tournament—no playing, no running, no nothing. At most, a few stretching exercises.

7. Above all, do your own thing. Each player is a unique physiologic entity with different energy levels and endurance patterns. Don't let yourself be talked into someone else's system. It never hurts to experiment with new methods once in a while on a trial basis. But when the chips are down, if it doesn't feel right to you, go back to the system that works best for you.

THE INNER GAME

Concentration is the core of performance. Mental gymnastics of all sorts have been tried. California pro Jay Jones uses an electronic noisemaker inserted in one ear like a hearing aid, to blot out distractions from the crowd. Tim Gallwey, of *Inner Game of Tennis* fame, warns against falling prey to the destructive sequence of negativism: "I missed that backhand → I have no backhand → I am not a good player → I am no good altogether." His is a plea for positive thinking: observe but don't berate yourself.

Jack Nicklaus has the ability to block out the other world with such intensity that he wouldn't hear a cannon go off in the middle of his backswing. My own approach boils down to this:

Don't play games—play points.
Don't play points—play shots.
Don't play shots—just play one shot—*the next one.*

This isn't quite as elementary as it seems. It takes a certain degree of mental discipline to stop thinking about the score, or the shot you missed on the last point—or last week, for that matter. But it is crucial that you empty

No matter how intense the competition (and Brumfield and McCoy are two of the game's fiercest competitors), it's clear that FUN is the name of the game.

your mind and zero in on the next shot. The pattern is set at the beginning of the point, whether you serve or receive. I'm convinced that the average player displays the poorest concentration when he serves. His mind is chock-full of the wrong thoughts. Half the time he just mindlessly bangs the ball into play.

When Arnold Palmer was asked, in his heyday, what the toughest shot in golf was, his reply was, "The next one."

Throughout this discussion I've attempted to dissect the game of racquetball into its component parts, the parts into molecules, the molecules into atoms. But the whole of racquetball is far greater than the sum of its parts in terms of fun. Whether your object is to stay in shape, get a little exercise, face an intriguing challenge in logic, or perfect the fine art of gamesmanship, you just can't find a game that has so much to offer in pure fun. Let me conclude as I began: I love this game.

Have a great time.

Glossary

ACE: A serve that scores a point without being touched by the receiver.

AROUND-THE-WALL BALL (AWB): A defensive shot with the path of side wall → front wall → side wall → floor.

AVOIDABLE HINDER: Avoidable interference that results in automatic loss of the exchange.

BACK COURT: The rear quarter of the court.

BACKHAND: The stroke that's hit on the opposite side of the shooting arm.

BODY LANGUAGE: Movement of the arms, torso, and legs, prior to striking the ball, that might give a clue to the choice of shot.

BOTTOM BOARD: The lowest point on the front wall.

CEILING SHOT: Defensive shot with the path of ceiling → front wall → floor.

CENTER COURT: The area covered by 1–2 steps either side of the short line.

CROSS-COURT PASS: An offensive shot that passes the opponent on the opposite side.

CUT-OFF SHOT: A shot hit before the bounce; fly shot; volley.

DEFENSIVE SHOT: A shot hit with no immediate intention to end the exchange; usually a ceiling shot; Z-ball; AWB.

DOWN-THE-WALL PASS: An offensive shot that passes the opponent on the same side.

DRIVE SERVE: A low, hard serve.

DROP SHOT: A soft tap to the front wall.

EXCHANGE: The rally; the playing of alternating shots.

FAULT: An illegal serve hitting the ceiling, back wall, or two side walls before the floor, or failing to carry over the short line.

FLY SHOT: A shot hit before the bounce; cut-off shot; volley.

171

FOREHAND: The stroke hit on the same side as the shooting arm.

FRONT COURT: Area in front of the service line.

GARBAGE SERVE: A shoulder-high lob serve.

HINDER: Interference causing stoppage of play.

KILL SHOT: A shot that hits too low on the front wall to be retrieved before the second bounce.

KILLER: A player who tries an unusually high percentage of kill shots; shooter; gunner.

LOB: A soft, defensive shot.

OFFENSIVE SHOT: A shot intended to end the rally, usually a kill or pass.

PASSING SHOT: A shot that gets by the other player.

PINCH SHOT: A kill shot that hits the side wall first.

PUMPKIN: A setup.

RABBIT: A player who is an exceptionally good retriever.

RALLY: The exchange; the playing of alternating shots.

REVERSE BACK-WALL SHOT: A shot hit into the back wall with enough force to carry to the front wall before the bounce.

REVERSE PINCH SHOT: A kill shot that hits the front wall, then the side wall, then the floor.

ROLLOUT: A kill shot that hits the absolute lowest point of the front wall.

SCREEN BALL: A visual hinder causing stoppage of play.

SERVE: The first shot of the rally.

SERVE RETURN: The first shot by the receiver.

SERVICE BOX: The area between the service line and the short line.

SERVICE LINE: The forward horizontal line, 15 feet from the front wall, which limits the server's forward motion.

SETUP: A return that gives a player a good chance to end the point with his next shot.

SHOOTER: A player who tries an unusually high percentage of kill shots; a killer; a gunner.

SHORT LINE: The horizontal line at mid-court, halfway between the front and back walls; the line the serve must pass over before the bounce.

SIDE-OUT: Loss of serve.

SKIP-BALL: A kill-shot attempt that hits the floor before the front wall.

STRAIGHT KILL: A kill shot that hits only the front wall.

V-BALL: A cross-court passing shot that hits the side wall as it goes by the player.

VOLLEY: A shot hit before the bounce; fly shot; cut-off shot.

WALLPAPER BALL: A shot that hugs the side wall.

WINNER: A shot that ends the rally; usually a kill shot or passing shot.

Z-BALL: A defensive shot with the path of front wall → side wall → side wall → floor.

Z-SERVE: A serve with the path of front wall → side wall → floor.